RONALD DUNCAN

THE MAN AND THE ARTIST

Ronald Duncan
the Man
and the Artist

KRYSIA CAIRNS

University of Plymouth

1998

First published in 1998 by
The University of Plymouth,
Exmouth, Devon, EX8 2AT

Copyright © 1998
Krysia Cairns

Photographs and published material
copyright © 1998
The Ronald Duncan Literary Foundation

Unpublished material copyright © 1998
Miranda Weston-Smith, Literary Executor
to the Estate of Ronald Duncan

Typeset by Country Setting
Woodchurch, Kent TN26 3TB
and printed and bound by
The Short Run Press Limited, Exeter EX2 7LW

ISBN 1 84102 000 1

1001276654

To James, William
and Edward Heather-Hayes,
my long-suffering sons,
who bore Mum being a student
with amazing tolerance and good humour

Acknowledgements

I would like to express my gratitude to Rose Marie Duncan, who fed and entertained me during my research at Home Farm; Robert Gee, for his interest and encouragement; and Anna Trussler, for her supportive expertise. The manuscripts here reproduced have been made available by courtesy of Miranda Weston-Smith, Literary Executor to the Estate of Ronald Duncan. My acknowledgements and thanks are also due to the Ronald Duncan Literary Foundation for making possible the publication of this work, as well as other postgraduate research on the poet and related literary enterprises. The archives of the Foundation have for the past three years been held at the Exmouth campus of the University of Plymouth, where this notable collection of the writer's literary manuscripts and memorabilia, the largest repository of Duncan documentation in existence, is now accessible for research into a wide range of subjects ranging from twentieth-century poetry and drama to opera, pacifist politics and self-sufficiency. *A Handlist of the Ronald Duncan Papers: the New Collection*, compiled by Anna Trussler (University of Plymouth, 1995), is held by most UK and European Universities .

Contents

A Highly Personal Foreword

Ronald Duncan, writer and farmer, had penetrating and luminous eyes set in a swarthy, gaunt and otherwise unremarkable face which dominated his small and carelessly dressed person. This picture remains vividly in my memory, as does the apprehension I felt at meeting for the first time – indeed the only time – the father of my friend Briony. This discomfort was due to a set of circumstances which must be recounted in order to explain my reasons for wanting to investigate the life and works of this less than well-known author primarily from a biographical viewpoint. Duncan had strong views concerning critical methods and I court his displeasure in this endeavour.

The work of Ronald Duncan needs fuller investigation, both academic and biographical, than is possible here. His many books lie unread and out of print, his plays out of fashion and unperformed. Academic interest alone can hope to save his considerable contribution to English literature from obscurity. As the Earl of Portsmouth said, 'He is too remarkable not to attract a biographer of substance in due course, as time justifies the pathways of his mind and the purpose of his living.' [1]

Duncan's widow, Rose-Marie, lived her life always in the shadow of her late husband – or as she describes the situation more aptly, 'on the periphery'. Yet she is herself a talented artist with an understanding and tolerance of the artistic temperament — in Colin Wilson's words, 'a complex character who deserves a biography to herself'.[2]

Briony and I became friends in the early years of our respective marriages, when nappies festooned our horizons. Such years are not without their heartbreak. Briony shouldered the burden of her parents' then current unhappiness, loving and loyal to both. In order to prepare her as gently as possible for the contents of her father's third volume of autobiography, *Obsessed*,[3] which she feared would be especially hurtful to her family, Briony gave me the book to read. The experience was to initiate in me a greater understanding of her situation.

I found *Obsessed* riveting. It is well written, with easy, flowing, confident and often poetic use of language, incorporating an element of waspishness which intrigued and startled me. I then read the two preceding volumes of autobiography, *All Men are Islands*[4] and *How to Make Enemies*,[5] which are similarly composed; often pretentious, with far-fetched or much exaggerated anecdotes, and over-obsessed with the 'self'. These books, to be examined later in this study, brought alive to me the man, his home and the frailties of love and life. I found myself looking with new eyes at my friend, at her bookshelves, at the poetry of Ezra Pound and T. S. Eliot, as if they themselves had emerged from the pages of an incredible fairy tale.

Later, in response to and sympathy with my unhappiness and despair at my husband's faithlessness, Briony turned to her father for advice on how best to comfort me. In character, he telephoned me several times urging me to wait, to sit it out, to be a mother and a sister to my spouse, 'as males were but frail creatures tossed like flotsam and jetsam in the tide of their desires'. Love, he told me, should not be possessive, and, as he said to William B. Wahl, 'the symbol of love should be two open hands – and let go'.[6] This old hand at adultery calmed me with his eloquence, flattered me with his concern. Hence my apprehension at meeting him at a later date. I felt that I knew him through his writing, the eyes of his daughter and his disembodied voice, but I became tongue-tied, overwhelmed by shyness. The questions I should like to have asked drowned in my memory, and the illusion of intimacy was shattered.

This all happened many years ago, but Briony and I remain close friends. I frequently stay with Rose-Marie, whom John Moat cites as 'the poet's wife';[7] and I talk to Karina, Ronnie's granddaughter, of his work as she prepares to undertake for a GCSE project an investigation into the forgotten works of her grandfather. Duncan's eyes pierce from his portraits by Rose-Marie, from behind the face of Rose-Marie in a composite portrait of her by Rebecca Cohen, and from sculptures sculpted by Briony and Epstein at Home Farm and West Mill. These seem to compel me to do what little I can to ward off the literary oblivion Duncan feared.

Further education can be the valium or the panacea of the deserted wife. Mature students who seek refuge in the academic, for one reason or another, are both advantaged and disadvantaged in a variety of ways. The seeking of the self is a bitter-sweet experience in life, and literature mirrors and enhances experience where all has gone before and nothing is new. One searches for identification with situation and emotion, or hopes for clues to the discovery of the self. This acts both as a release and an impediment to freedom of expression. Experience of life, especially reflected in poetry, is at once a pain and a pleasure, almost too personal to be shared even between pen and paper. The work of Ronald Duncan has contributed to my long-sought conclusion that there are no answers to life. We never really 'know' ourselves: we change with the wind, therefore we can never 'really know' one another. Life exists only in the past and in the future. Duncan looks for 'self' – is indeed, on his own admission, obsessed with it – and the seeking is a path of discovery he shares with his all too few readers.

It is my personal knowledge of this man, and those whose lives he influenced, that has led me to read and appreciate much of his work. This intimacy has enhanced my enjoyment of that which I would have enjoyed anyway, but has contributed an air of the romantic which we more usually look for in fiction. My strongest plea against the argument advanced by Duncan in Chapter One is that bio-graphical detail enhances my pleasure and my under-standing of Duncan the man and the writer – but only in the manner of the following of clues in a maze. I draw no solid conclusions, my intellect seeks no concrete answers. I strive to interest the reader in the work of this author.

As Colin Wilson suggests, 'all Duncan's work springs out of his complexity as a human being. And fortunately he has handed us the key to some of this complexity' in his autobiographies. [8]

Introduction

This study is an investigation of Ronald Duncan, the man and the artist. A recurrent theme is the role and practice of criticism and the validity of the biographical approach – this is in spite of Duncan's own views on this method of criticism, which will be discussed in detail.

In Chapter One the concept of the biographical approach in relation to the role and function of criticism is considered through the views of Eliot, Pound and Duncan and the more modern critics Helen Gardner, Cleanth Brookes and Colin Wilson.

Chapter Two is a continuation of some of the arguments expounded in the first chapter, and a concentrated critical commentary on Duncan's poetry. Use is made of his ideas on form in recognition of the fact that poetry, of all literary genres, has the strongest case for the right to be criticised without recourse to biographical detail. While respecting Duncan's view that 'what he [the poet] is communicating is the prime factor', Duncan the man is also considered.

Chapter Three explores the significance of Duncan's autobiographies and is concerned with the close inter-relationship between Duncan the man and Duncan the artist. In this chapter and the following, which together explore Duncan's journalistic, instructional, fictional and dramatic writing, I feel freer in using the autobiographical approach. The three autobiographies examined reveal that

Duncan drew constantly upon his own life and experiences as subject matter, and also the extent to which his friends, family, loves and environment influenced him. They reveal Duncan's self-indulgence yet also the 'deflatory' approach noted by Colin Wilson in Chapter One.

I move next to a consideration of Duncan as a prolific writer of great complexity and range, examining each area of his extensive output. One of the limitations encountered in this study, where such a wealth of material might have been used, is the inevitable tendency to 'list' much material, simply to make apparent to the reader the range and complexity of the work of this prolific writer.

In the final chapter, my major area of concern is Duncan's drama and the effects of criticism – the aim here not being directed solely at. attempting to establish the validity of the biographical approach in examining Duncan's work, but also to suggest a degree of justification for his later bitterness towards the critics; to reveal his initial popularity and success as a playwright, and the need to acknowledge and pay tribute to his lasting contribution to the English stage.

Published and unpublished works have been used, with some of the latter reproduced as appendixes. Private papers and personal diaries are referred to and quoted from with the kind permission of Mrs Rose-Marie Duncan and the Trustees of the Ronald Duncan Literary Foundation.

I

Criticism and Biography

Duncan had strong views on the role and practice of criticism. In some notes for a planned book on English literature he states:

> The poet's own personality, his own psychic diffi-
> culties or amorous entanglements are, in the last
> analysis, frivolous and trivial. But today Personality
> is at a premium. Even the most serious scholars in
> literature find themselves mere gossip columnists on
> the Hills of Parnassus. And we have reached that
> point where the life of a poet is more important than
> his poetry. I believe that a poem is a communication,
> not a decoration, an urgent communication and not
> a casual postcard on the back of a pretty view. I use
> the word communication advisedly, a moment of
> communion (the centre of religious experience of
> spiritual growth), and a poem is a point of growth
> within our consciousness. What he [the poet] is
> communicating is the prime factor. The poem, the
> thing expressed, must be lucid, it must cohere.
> The value of being is in the consciousness. The
> world is dark, poetry is the light in it.
>   Art and poetry must be about something, con-
> vey something, and can be judged firstly by the
> content, the value of its statement and secondly,

the effectiveness with which it says it. This is the
keel of criticism and criticism deserves to sink if it
is without these two criteria. [1]

These beliefs, or statements, provide a focus for discussion in this study. Tied in with these assertions is the
complex question of biographical detail. Duncan's mentors
and friends, Ezra Pound and T. S. Eliot, have views which
he may have discussed with them.

Eliot questions how far biographical information helps
in the understanding of poetry, but expands to add that
such detail may be more important in the case of one poet
and less in that of another. However, he warns that too
much information may break one's contact with the poem.
Thus, all methods of criticism have their limitations and
dangers, especially since individual interpretation, understanding and appreciation of a work of literature is complex and varied.

Eliot believed that biographical detail was not relevant
to the understanding of poetry, since poetry 'cannot be
explained in terms of something else'.

Perhaps the form of criticism in which the dangers
of excessive reliance upon causal explanation is
greatest is the critical biography, especially when the
biographer supplements his knowledge of external
facts with psychological conjectures about inner
experience. I do not suggest that the personality and
the private life of a dead poet constitute sacred
ground on which the psychologist must not tread. . . .
Nor is there any reason why biographies of poets

should not be written. Furthermore, the biographer
of an author should possess some critical ability; he
should be a man of taste and judgement, appreciative
of the work of the man whose biography he
undertakes. And on the other hand any critic
seriously concerned with a man's work should be
expected to know something about the man's life. [2]

Duncan wrote: 'Ezra Pound taught me more in one day
than I had learned in a year at Cambridge' [3] (where F. R.
Leavis was his respected tutor from whom he learned a
great deal). Also: 'If I have any knowledge of that craft
[poetry writing] myself, I owe it more to Ezra Pound's
blue pencil, and to Eliot's comments and queries in the
margin than to the lectures of Mrs Bennett or Dr
Tillyard.'[4] In this Duncan shows a greater respect for the
practitioners than the teachers.

Greatly influenced by Pound and Eliot, Duncan shared
their view that formalist criticism should be concerned
primarily with the work itself. Pound goes yet further in
believing that one should

. . . pay no attention to the criticism of men who
have never themselves written a notable work.
Consider the discrepancies between the actual
writing of the Greek poets and dramatists and
the theories of the Graeco-Roman grammarians,
concocted to explain their metres. [5]

Eliot [6] considered Johnson to be one of the three greatest
critics of poetry in English literature – Dryden and

Coleridge being the other two. All are poets. He places
Johnson in the position of a secondary poet at the end of a
movement initiated by greater ones. Dryden and Coleridge
both represent something new in the poetry of their time.
This does appear to confirm Pound's belief that poetry
should only be judged by poets. The criticism of scholars
appears to be entirely redundant to these masters.

In the Introduction to his *Selected Lyrics and Satires of the
Earl of Rochester*, Duncan states:

> . . . what biographical facts I set down here are,
> I know, largely irrelevant in evaluating the poet's
> work. Experiences do not describe an artist; an artist
> describes his experience. . . . In short, what I am
> trying to do here is to persuade people to read
> Rochester's poetry rather than go off satisfied with
> my opinion of him. A great deal of so-called literary
> (and musical) criticism now consists of nothing
> more than a parlour game 'Hunt the Origin' or
> 'Face the Influence'. All of which helps to cover
> many paragraphs and eventually trains the mind
> to a proper appreciation of detective novels.

Duncan derides the 'passion to pigeon-hole poets', especially among those who like talking about but not reading
poetry. [7] His views, embodying those of Pound and Eliot,
on the role and practice of literary criticism deny the
biographical approach in the evaluation of a poet's work.
This denial is enlarged upon in Chapter Two.

In 1923, in his now famous article 'The Function of
Criticism', [8] Eliot felt that the essential function of literary

criticism was the 'elucidation of works of art, and the correction of taste'. In 1956, in the Gideon Seymour Lecture delivered at the University of Minnesota (and later published by that institution), he changed his mind. The essential function was to 'promote the understanding and enjoyment of literature' – the understanding was more important than the explanation. One should be wary of the purely explanatory critic. Criticism is not a science.

In the opinion of Colin Wilson (writer, 'angry young man' of the 1950s, author of *The Outsider* and a friend of Duncan), in agreement here with Eliot, knowledge of the personality and life of some poets adds to the enjoyment and understanding of their work. There are basically two kinds of writers – 'personalities and non-personalities'. He lists Eliot with Aldous Huxley and W. H. Auden in the 'non-personality' group, and Dr Johnson, Hemingway, Dylan Thomas and Duncan in that in which 'personality' adds dimension to their writings. He claims that Duncan 'deflates' himself in his work, as in his parody of Whitman in *The Solitudes*.[9]

> To my essential self – I sing –
> Not to the I,
> Man of the hat, coat and tie:
> But to the me,
> – coffee, muddle and misery. [10]

In agreement with Colin Wilson, all Duncan's work is 'deeply autobiographical'. Duncan uses his own weaknesses and his own self-indulgence in his works, and this is the strength of his poetry and drama especially. Further comments are made in Chapter Three on Wilson's description of Duncan's autobiographies as 'a deliberate red herring'.

Whilst in agreement with Cleanth Brookes that 'speculation' on the mental processes of the author takes the critic away from the work into biography and psychology, and should not be confused with an account of the work, and that a reduction of a work of literature to its causes does not constitute literary criticism,[11] the argument can be taken further for the purposes of this investigation, bearing in mind Colin Wilson's observation that biographical detail used in a supplementary manner, without unfounded 'speculation', can only heighten the reader's awareness and appreciation of Duncan's work.

2

Poetry and Ronald Duncan's Views on Form

Kenneth Burke has suggested that poetry should be analysed solely by formal criteria, without reference to the personality or biographical background of the author. [1] In this 'the Formalist critic fulfils his "proper" task by imputing to the work whatever designs, or intention, he thinks is best able to account for the nature of the work'. Burke makes a valid point when he says that the biographical approach, in the case of poetry, returns the text from literature to the 'every day'.

In Duncan's words, as quoted previously, 'What he [the poet] is communicating is the prime factor.' The poet, reducing the verbosity of everyday speech, has already sifted out and discarded that which no longer matters, so as to emphasise what is of importance in his communication. Extracts from Duncan's poem, 'Poetry', articulate this:

The word, a swipe at the jungle,
the inarticulate undergrowth;
the right word; a sharp sickle
precisely fashioned:
as 'scythe' conveys the sweep of a blade. . . .
words can create, not merely describe,
They extend the keyboard of consciousness. . . .
Words are the torch poets use
to lighten up the cavern of your own being [2]

F. R. Leavis holds that 'the way in which the poet uses language is the central criteria of how he feels'. Sincerity of expression is genuine and 'no [biographical] facts about the poet can of themselves make it insincere'. He claims too, that inner states are essentially expressed and judged in terms of objective qualities; there is no room for essentially private emotions and subjective responses.[3]

Helen Gardner [4] comments, in the preface to her scholarly study of and commentary on the texts and drafts of Eliot's *Four Quartets*, that 'the study of the creative process, however interesting, has far less to give than a study of the object created' – that her labour only increased her understanding and enjoyment of Eliot's work.[5] Yet, as Colin Wilson points out, Eliot belongs to the 'non-personality' class of poet, being an unemotional and highly moral man.

In his comments on *Dante the Maker*, by William Anderson, Duncan begins:

Here we are again: another book about a poet, 500 pages at £18 while the poet himself goes unread and is out of print. But what does that matter? Scholars need subjects and PhD's breed PhD's. And Mr. Anderson has been a most assiduous mole; he has burrowed hard, worked hard, as his bibliography proves, but it is all academia; no poetry surfaces. [6]

In Duncan's introduction to Dante, *De Vulgari Eloquentia* (the publication of which he undertook at his own expense in the hope of encouraging people to read Dante), he points out that,

Apart from Poe's excellent essay on his composition
of 'The Raven', and this thesis of Dante's, there is
so very little written on the techniques of poetry
on HOW it is written as opposed to WHAT it is about.
I suspect that critics are content with the latter,
poets themselves are interested in the former. . . .
We are a literate nation and so long as we have
books about poets, there is no need to read the
sods themselves. [7]

These views confirm that poetry, of all forms of literature,
makes the strongest case for the right to criticism without
recourse to biographical detail. Duncan embarked upon the
English Tripos having already decided that he would be
a poet. After three years he 'had little knowledge of any
literary form or of the technicalities of poetry'. His lecture
notes were

littered with irrelevant dates of the poets' lives,
but nobody thought it worth while to instruct us
how to make a canzone, or even inform us about
the intricacies of the sestina or sonnet. Many
who get a first in the Tripos could not answer the
most elementary questions on prosody or metric.
Biographical details clutter their predatory minds. [8]

As a concession to, and in agreement with, many of these
views on biographically-based investigation of poetry, the
use of Duncan's 'The Ars Poetae'[9] as a criterion by which
poetry can be viewed may be justified. Technically, the
use of this unpublished paper, which contains some of

Duncan's views on poetry, is to resort to 'biographical detail' as an aid in the evaluation of some of his poetry. The paper originated as a crib for a young girl taking 'A'-levels. Duncan describes poetry as being 'communication from one part of his mind to another – to which we are privileged to eavesdrop'.[10] Here we 'eavesdrop' on his views of poetry.

> What is poetry? It is a communication . . . not
> necessarily from the poet to the people [but also]
> from the poet's perception to his own under-
> standing. . . . It can only be judged by assessing the
> validity or truth of what the poem says and the
> effectiveness with which it says it. Poetry is Not
> mere decoration to thought or embroidery upon the
> structure of drama. Not an effusion like tea but
> the Essence i.e. the irreducible minimum. Not
> necessarily a pretty picture of an herbaceous border;
> a bloody sunset or a mere collection of images, rimes
> or regular or monotonous lines. . . . It does not exist
> in rimes or muddled metaphor. Not in ambiguities.
> Nor certainly as a trifle for 'leisure', [but] Poetry is
> the point
> > at which consciousness grows.
> > At which sensitivity seeks
> > It is the discovery of sensibility
> > Where thought and feeling
> > supported by experience and
> > observation *extend* our
> > range of living, perception.
> > A good poem adds to human experience.

It tells us something we didn't know before
didn't feel before
hadn't seen ourselves before
but after will know, feel and see for ourselves.
A Good Poem Adds to us

On the other 'and
a Bad Poem pretends to be what it ain't
Clothing itself in
2nd hand verbal clothing
poetical clutter
rimes
flowers
ambiguities
and muddle
It thinks nothing
Feels not for itself
And adds nowt to us.

Duncan continues in this vein, saying that poetry is not just a verbal pattern, since 'good coffee is a poem. Poetry is a creation' and 'may you be damned if you use poetry . . . as a thing apart from living'. He urges Briony (who was the 'A'-level student he was writing for) to make use of poetry 'which adds to you, which tells you something, and becomes an adjunct, an extension to yourself', and to discard that poem which does not. Duncan impresses on her how much is owed to the poet and poetry:

> . . . consider what you would think
> how much you would

feel
to whom
and how you'd pray
if he hadn't first
felt
shown
knelt
known
and showed you the way.

He concludes that:

Humanity, Madame, is of no consequence
except for its consciousness
and that consciousness
that awareness
that waking
has been in the poem
by the poem
and is the poem.

These views can be used as a framework for examining some of Duncan's poetry, as also can the opinions in his article on 'English Appreciation', an introduction to a projected book. They present an opportunity for compromise in the debate as to the role and practice of literary criticism. Pound, in his view that poetry should only be judged by poets, and Duncan, with his preference for the practitioner rather than the teacher of the Art of Poetry, would presumably not have objected to the use of these documents which lay down a poet's (in this case Duncan's) expectations of any poem. He can help in the criticism of his own poetry. As he says:

> One of the reasons why poetry is so little read today
> is that is has become irrelevant. It tells us little: that
> a rose is a rose is a rose as Gertrude Stein put it;
> it decorates perhaps but fails to enlarge the potentials
> of our being. Bad poetry can be merely pretty, great
> poetry must be painful and disturbing. Man gains
> from pain not pleasure. Good poetry should disturb.
> A great poem is something which makes us different
> than the person we were before reading it. [11]

Duncan's poem 'The Gift' [12] fulfils the requirement of being a communication, 'a discovery of sensibility where thoughts and feelings supported by experience and observation extend our range of living, perception' — it tells us something 'which I did not feel before, see for myself', but 'after will know, feel and see for myself':

> Since she whom I love
> has a gift for jealousy;
> I — a talent for adultery,
> We reached that point where
> We kept our friends in conversation;
> Lawyers in fees, and ourselves
> In something that passed for anger,
> But was more like grief.
>
> Now I see I must learn to love
> her jealousy;

it being part of her,
and hope that she can love me
for my adultery.
But this she's done. This she's done.
    could it be her jealousy was a gift,
A gift to me?
We have begun. It is not done.

Biographical research confirms that the 'she' is Rose-Marie and 'that point' was a stage in their marriage.

Although Helen Gardner found in her work on Eliot's *Four Quartets* that the study of the work itself was more rewarding, in this instance, where the author belongs to 'the personality' group, such is not the case. The awareness and appreciation of the work is enhanced by the knowledge that there was much soul-searching and months of unhappiness for both parties, in the seeking and realization of the conclusions arrived at in the poem. It is a communication 'from the poet's perception to his understanding' and it can be judged 'by assessing the validity or truth of what the poem says'; it is of greater value because it is of a true experience. The art of the poet has, by economy of language, the choice of words, the sounds and the punctuation, made a personal experience into one that is recognisable and universal. The pain of the progress to that conclusion is identifiable by the reader.

The word 'gift', not usually associated with jealousy, immediately alerts the reader to the depth of thought throughout the poem, as does the 'talent for adultery'. Both human failings become gifts, indicating the complexity of human emotion and the idea that man grows from pain, not pleasure. Divorce is portrayed as both anger and grief. Conciliation is concerned with loving faults as well as virtues, which is of reality and not the 'romance' of the perfect world. The repetition of 'This she's done' confirms forgiveness, acceptance and realisation on the one side, and the questioning on the other which leads to the rebirth of the relationship or marriage in 'it is not done'. Jealousy and adultery could be reconciled, having been aired as grievances.

The poem is written in free verse but with a disciplined, definite slow rhythm, denoting deep and serious thought leading to revelation and hope. This discovery is denoted by the movement from the longer, ponderous lines of the first stanza to the suggestion of a certain decisiveness and realisation in the shorter, repetitive lines of the second. The poem does indeed reveal the consciousness.

Duncan's poem 'Song'[13] is primarily a poem of sound, imagery and technique:

> In the forest of my dreams
> My fierce desire
> Tigers her movements.

> By the river that is sleep
> My slow eyes
> Serpent her breasts of light.

> Like a gorse bush that's on fire
> My quick blood
> Stallions her loins of night.

> Across the desert of the day
> My blind hands
> Weep for her presence.

The 'ss' sound is predominent, giving a slow, savage sense of articulated passions, of snake and prey, concise and lucid. The noun 'tiger' used in the form of a verb is startling in its effect, as are 'serpents' and 'stallions'. The imagery throughout the poem is direct and immensely evocative of sight, sound, light and darkness, as is the personification of 'blind hands' which 'weep for her presence'. This poem requires nothing outside itself to be fully appreciated.

In 'Words',[14] Duncan wrote that 'a noun that is most active suggests a verb. For instance, the word tiger implies ferocity laying in wait for stalking, and the final spring.' 'He tigered his prey' obtains 'greater immediacy' than 'he lay in wait for his prey like a tiger'. Duncan uses, as Wahl suggests, 'the metaphor in a sense adjectivally rather than using it in the standard metaphor form' – an 'impacted metaphor', as Duncan himself called it, which avoids the use of *like*, 'as in a thing being *like* another thing – but rather making IT a thing', thus cutting out clumsy metaphoric convention.[15]

Later, in 'Words', Duncan expands his ideas. 'If the verb is right, the rest of the sentence is driven to meaning. . . . Every word is a metaphor for a thing or a condition of a thing. . . . But a verb gives the thing being (to be – derives from the Aryan – to grow).' In an attempt to make the sentence 'Autumn like a pheasant's tail lifts over the hedge' more creative, he suggests 'Pheasant Autumn lifts over the hedge', which achieves

a noun in which the metaphor is implied. But we
have lost the explicit connection between the colours
of autumn and the colour of the pheasant's tail. But
this connection is no great loss in meaning, for it is
impossible to think of Autumn or pheasant without
visualising their colours.

The sentence becomes 'Pheasant-Autumn tails over the
hedge', in which

the new verb gives the visual image. But the sentence
is still not perfect i.e. carrying the maximum charge
of meaning within the minimum number of words.
. . . The new compound noun is clumsy . . . let us
concentrate our metaphor wholly within the act,
within the verb and write 'Autumn pheasants over
the hedge'. But even now we can achieve greater
concision because the preposition is implicit within
the verb. We all know not only a pheasant's
colouring but how the bird moves too. Therefore
it is possible to drive the sentence to 'Autumn
pheasants the hedge' and give the metaphor wholly
in charge of the verb.

This confirms Duncan's belief that 'Poetry is that language
which can carry the maximum charge. It is language at its
most intense.'[16] The effectiveness of this conviction has
been seen in the technique of the poem 'Song'.

The particular appeal of Duncan's work lies in its
directness and lucidity, and the sense of 'communication'
achieved through the sound, rhythm and imagery. Pound

spoke of three kinds of poetry: the Melopoeia with its musical properties; the Phanopoeia, or the casting of images upon the visual imagination; and Logopoeia, or that of aesthetic content, particularly in the 'domain of verbal manifestation'; Duncan's poetry possesses some of these properties.[17] This is not a claim for the originality of his approach, which is in the tradition of Eliot, Pound, Auden and Hopkins as well as of Cavalcanti, Dante and Rochester. Duncan was himself aware of this, believing most poetry to be plagiaristic in that all poets use the medium of words.

Strong as Duncan's views are on the use of biographical detail in the analysis, criticism and appreciation of poetry, he appears to be anxious to 'tell' of his techniques to Wahl, in his autobiographies and in his many articles on literature.[18] In *Obsessed* he writes:

> Why do I disclose our precious intimacy and privacy? I write only for you, for us. I will censor nothing. Ronald Duncan lived here. I am ashamed not of my life, only of my death. Having written my own life honestly, no grubbing journalist or assiduous PhD will dare to invent what I've already exposed. When the fox hangs himself he is at least saved from the hounds. [19]

Such comments and articles as the ones so far quoted remove the mystery of technique and purpose which shrouds the work of so many writers and which give rise to so much debate and vastly differing interpretations. In the case of Duncan, we are encouraged to lift the veil of the craftsmanship in order to engage readily with the 'consciousness' of the poem.

On his own admission, Duncan was captivated by the sound of words — but music, too, was important.[20] He experimented in writing poetry to obtain some of the effects found in music. He avoided 'the rhythm or voice being terminated or dropped by the terrible dead wall of full stops', which resulted in the excessive use of the colon; dropped it in revolt against the 'stream of consciousness diarrhoea of James Joyce', and reverted to clarity and order. Duncan destroyed all his experimental poems.[21] He was nauseated by free verse (the then current mode) and the 'lack of ability to submit to and write within a form'.[22]

He said to Wahl that 'a poet must know how to write all the forms and then he can break the rules'.[23] Yet technical expertise is not enough. Poets must have other interests besides poetry in order to have anything to write about, to turn experience into thought and thence into poetry. The critic, too, must not only be a technical expert.

Several poems have been chosen here in order to portray the range, versatility and extent of Duncan's poetical works. Published collections include *Selected Poems*[24] and *The Solitudes*.[25] The latter is a collection selected and published by Eliot from poems written to Virginia Maskell (Duncan's mistress) on postcards during one of their separations.[26] These are intensely passionate and personal, concerning both wife and mistress. In this selection is included a short poem which to my mind might serve as Duncan's epitaph:

> Oblivion as a writer,
> Death as a man;
> This is your future;
> Escape it if you can.

Eliot suggested that the works included in *Unpopular Poems* should be omitted from *The Solitudes* as they were 'not good enough'.[27] On the cover of this small volume is printed: 'Ronald Duncan has never belonged to any school of writing and never felt obliged to swim with the tide of fashion or fad' – hence the title. The label 'the lone wolf of English Literature' was given to Duncan by Ezra Pound.[28]

For the Few is a mixture of poems easily identifiable as being related to his life. It includes such titles as 'For Rose-Marie's Birthday', 'Lines for My Daughter on her Wedding Day', 'In Delhi' – and 'The Poet', who

> with some temerity . . . explored
> the dark labyrinths of his own mind
> and from its complexity
> brought back simplicity:
> discovering the God who lies in a pail of milk . . .
> Though his map leads you nowhere but where
>   you are.

Although these poems are so personally titled, they are still primarily 'communications' – from within the poet to his audience – of simple feeling and experiences which are of universal application and implication. They need no recourse to biographical detail to explain them, only to enhance their validity because they derive from true experiences.

'Judas' is a long, poignant poem published as a volume, deeply reverent and 'religious' by this agnostic poet.[29] Religion is returned to in the last chapter in the context of 'religio' – which means 'to connect'.

Man, published in five volumes, is Duncan's last and perhaps the greatest of his published poetical works, presenting a vast but rewarding undertaking for the critical student or reader. In this volume Duncan turns away from the personal, saying,

> I realised that what I had to do was not to write
> the conventional autobiography before me, but to
> attempt a poem which would trace the emergent
> consciousness in man. My concern with anthro-
> pology led me to biology; biology to geology;
> geology to physics; my concern with physics to
> psychology, taking a hint from Heisenberg who has
> remarked that the observer cannot be separated
> from the observed. I found I was, and in my forties
> scientifically illiterate. From asking where I came
> from, I was led to ask myself where the earth came
> from. . . . [I found] poetry in science. . . . I cannot
> distinguish between them. [30]

Duncan focuses on physics and cosmology; on molecular biology and anthropology; on the evolution of man; on inventions which moved the consciousness forward; and on the nature of consciousness and its potential. Colin Wilson suggests that '*Man* is undoubtedly Duncan's greatest work, the work by which he will be judged.'

> It must also rank as one of the most ambitious
> poems every written, in this century or any other. . . .
> After the intensely personal heel of *The Solitudes*, the
> disappointing cul-de-sac of the theatre, [Duncan]
> had stumbled upon a theme that liberated all his
> imaginative energy and that allowed him to direct
> it into his most ambitious creative enterprise.

Wilson cites *Man* as 'one of the most exciting and boldly conceived works of literature'. Had Wilson written his essay without the evidence he found in *Man*, or if Duncan had died before he had written it, Wilson would have continued to feel that Duncan was a 'personal writer' in the sense 'that the personal life and work are so closely interwoven that one cannot be understood without the other'. However, *Man* demanded 'revision of this estimate' in that 'it reveals that he has brought under control and learned to utilise the enormous subconscious forces that seemed to threaten to destroy him. The work has the vitality of a volcanic upheaval.' Wilson feels that Duncan has succeeded where Pound and Charles Olsen failed with the casual and formless qualities of their work, and that *Man*, which is arguably Duncan's most remarkable contribution to English literature,

> should do for Duncan what the later Cantos did for
> Pound; reveal him as one of the most interesting and
> important writers of his generation. I think it would
> amuse him to become a Grand Old Man of Letters.
> It will surely be the most unlikely disguise he has
> assumed so far.[31]

Because this study concerns itself with Duncan, the man and his work, more detailed discussion of *Man* as a remarkable piece of English literature is not relevant here. The period of its creation, the latter part of Duncan's life, is the subject of an as yet unpublished, possibly fourth volume of autobiography, *The Precarious Garden*. Duncan's reasons for turning away from the 'self' towards 'the poetry of science', anticipated therein, would have been of value to this study (without affecting the poetical content and worth of his work as 'literature'). Although the manuscript has been located, it is as yet unavailable for reference. *Man* is only one of the important developments in the last decade of his life, and a great deal of bitterness and disillusionment permeates Duncan's being and thinking in these later years. Satire, anger and the fear of 'oblivion as a writer' dominate his last works, which are all, as yet, unpublished.

The Mongrel,[32] Duncan's first published collection of poetry, is an important factor at this point in the debate and requires some highlighting. Duncan often refers to the lines, 'It rained behind my eyes . . . the river of sadness flowing inside me', and confesses that for many years he had 'tried to evade this centre of [my] being trying to objectify it. . . . I believe I got somewhere near it in "The Mongrel".' He also confesses to having repeated over and over again in his poems the line, 'All day I've been trying to forget what I dared not remember; and all day I've been trying to remember what I could not forget.'

To Wahl he said: 'I've always been haunted by the fact that there are things I cannot remember, which I daren't remember. The key to all this is in the poem called "The Mongrel".'[33] Although such directions offered by poets are of debatable value, in this case it would appear to be indicating that *Man* evolved from the line of thinking expressed in Duncan's first book of poetry published in 1950. Technically it is less than perfect when compared with the sophistication of *Man*. 'The Mongrel' does, however, demonstrate that Duncan progressed both as poet and human being.

'The Mongrel', a poem of forty three stanzas divided into three parts of differing lengths, and written in the strict verse form of the canzone, takes the shape of a monologue, with thought interrupted by associations and memories. It is a questioning, deeply emotional and highly autobiographical work, with many of Duncan's characteristics of craftsmanship, thoughts and ideas. It is indeed an attempt to 'objectify the centre of his being'.

The first part serves as an introduction to the second, and concerns inherited memory, or the knowledge or instinct of the jungle of tiger, panther and viper, and touches upon the subject of human reincarnation. These stanzas are crafted with a sensitive use of alliteration, as in:

> Does the terror of the tiger's tooth
> Tear through a horse's dream?

> 'Till all the world is woven in her web
> and the wind is held by the frail sails of silken
>   industry

The poem demonstrates, too, Duncan's economic use of powerful, thought-provoking imagery and verbal invention, as in 'as with cautious paw it treads the night'.

Part Two involves the reader in the similar, parallel human predicament and is concerned with the problem of the nature of reality, posing the question:

> What is our life but a slow remembering?
> What is our death but a quick forgetting?

Duncan ponders the problem of personal identity without reaching a concrete conclusion. The tone is rhetorical and introspective. He confesses that his poem is muddled and all very mystic.

Part Three begins: 'The present is where we are, but where are we?' And the lines

> What with time tied to our tail, teasing us,
> As we attempt the tightrope and step from the
> narrow womb into the narrow grave,
> Immortal — as the ash we burned into the carpet.

give the reader an image of life as the poet sees it, but which is not the answer he seeks. The act of seeking is the one of importance. The mongrel is in fact Christ, whose 'memory' he runs from and is pursued by. Christ's mercy is likened to the unwanted mongrel, grateful for any show of affection or attention.

'The Mongrel' is a strange poem which achieved a mixed reception. The opinion of Richard Murphy was derogatory, accusing the volume of being

> composed according to the modern convention of
> experiment, novelty and farce. Yet the new idioms

and forms, which liberated the early styles of Mr
Pound and Mr Eliot from the exhausted conventions
of the last century, have now themselves imposed a
convention on our literature, and the bondage of this
fashion, as well as the decay into which its standards
are fallen, are apparent in this volume. [34]

Duncan's style and form in the title poem do reveal 'the
exhausted conventions of the last century', and the use of
Greek subtitles and Eliot's technique of interrupting his
own attempts to explain himself perhaps validate the latter
part of Murphy's criticism. However, 'the exhausted conventions' of the last century are, in context, adding to the
author's discourse on his remembered past. Duncan's personal interjections are not mere imitation of Eliot, but an
honest part of his 'objectifying' process.

The critic Joan Blacksell believes that in 'The Mongrel'
Duncan

poses the poignant problem of the nature of reality.
There is a need to participate through actual, remembered or imagined experience in the common human
situation, and having taken part, to take responsibility for it, and then to ponder his own identity. [35]

This meandering poem does just that: it participates
through actual, remembered or imagined experience. As the
critic of *The Times Literary Supplement* concluded: 'This
monologue, now shrugging, now swept with questioning
and deep emotion, is a curiously rich and well controlled
vehicle for its theme.'[36]

According to Colin Wilson, Duncan was prone to absent-mindedness – and 'remembering' and 'forgotten' are key words in 'The Mongrel'. Wilson describes this tendency as

> a rather odd kind of absent-mindedness . . . of an altogether more exalted order . . . to the point of dottiness [which in Duncan] seems to be so much more bizarre that one can only assume it has some subconscious origin – that the romantic in him rejects the everyday world so completely that he sometimes behaves as if it did not exist.[37]

It would appear that Duncan really did feel a perpetual sense of *déja vu*. This poem is a genuine attempt to objectify the centre of his being, 'to ponder his own identity', and biographical knowledge does, in this case, help towards its understanding; making it perhaps less 'strange' by drawing to the reader's attention that it is the *act of seeking* which is the important issue here.

The central themes of Duncan's poetry which extend into his other works of literature are: the conflicting self; love – the egotistical, the possessive, the amorous and the selfless (Christ); the limits of the human mind and the realities of man's pain, suffering and loneliness. These themes are also the fundamental issues or concerns of Duncan's life, his living and his experiences, confirming the absolute involvement of Duncan as man and artist.

Poetry was, according to his family, the most personally important aspect of Duncan's work. More time and space has therefore been devoted to this area than can be allocated to his other literary works. His preoccupation with and love for poetry and language led him into the field of poetic drama and to some success as a verse dramatist, and this is the subject of Chapter Five. In this area, biographical detail can be more freely used as a vehicle of discovery in order to appreciate the nature of Duncan's contribution to the English theatre.

3
The Significance of Duncan's Autobiographies

D uncan's three volumes of autobiography reveal the close interrelationship between the man and the artist. The first page of these volumes prepares the reader for an experience quite outside the well-trodden path of the usual episodic autobiography. *All Men are Islands* begins:

> We settle down to write our life when we no
> longer know how to live it. To pause is to admit
> defeat. When the present is interesting we do
> not bother with the past. We try to remember
> it only when we've lost the vitality of doing
> anything worth remembering. The past is a waste-
> paper basket. We burrow into it only when we
> have no future.

In *How to Make Enemies* Duncan states:

> An autobiography cannot give an accurate picture of
> a man's life if it is to be readable. . . . An accurate
> autobiography would never find a publisher; if it did,
> it would never hold a reader.[1]

And *Obsessed* begins:

> Damn, blast and bugger. I don't want to write this.
> For five years I've been trying not to write this. Why

do I do so now? Because I have no option. Because
murderers are compelled to return to the scene of
their crime. Because grief is a burden . . . writing
this can only undo and damage me. . . . As for the
'gentle reader' he can take a running jump up
himself. I write this for you alone.

Within these openings, reminiscent of the expectations of
a novel written in the first person singular, lies the promise
of ruthless self-revelation; of a 'good read'; of pitiless self-
questioning. These autobiographies, outlining chronologi-
cally an unusual and complex life, are indeed for the most
part a racy read.

Duncan was born in Rhodesia in 1914, prematurely by
Caesarean operation after his mother had been charged by a
bull. His father's surname was Dunkelsbühler, and he was a
bastard son of the Crown Prince of Bavaria. Brought up by
his mother in England, he enjoyed a privileged childhood
and education, financed by his father's mother, and this
allowed him to concentrate wholly upon his chosen career
of poet and writer. This is not to say that Duncan's works
were a mere indulgence. He earned his living by writing and
farming, but his start in life was such that his artistic spirit
was free from financial worry. This allowed him the freedom to investigate his own libido.

Early in Duncan's professional life he met, learned from
and enjoyed the company of such men as Pound, Eliot,
Benjamin Britten and Gandhi. (Duncan wrote a pamphlet
on non-violence in industrial disputes [2] which he sent to
the Mahatma, who then asked him to live with him at his
Ashram, in Wardha. Duncan accepted.) His frequent refer-

ences to such famous names can often appear pretentious, yet these people played a prominent part in Duncan's life and work.

When the autobiographies were written Duncan was part of this closely-knit literary and artistic circle. Such men were frequent visitors to his home at West Mill in its magical setting at Marsland Mouth – made famous by Charles Kingsley as the abode of the White Witch, Lucy Passmore: 'To landward, all richness, softness and peace; to seaward, a waste and howling wilderness of rock and roller.'[3] This environment was (and is) both a retreat for and a challenge to the artistic soul. It was appropriate to and a perfect background for this pacifist farmer-poet, with his love of the soil, of fish, and of beachcombing – and his phobia about death. Rose-Marie confirms the comradeship of Britten and others at West Mill with her memories of impromptu concerts, of Eliot's 'obsession with his bowels'[4] at her dinner parties, and of the stimulating company of George Harewood and so many notables.

It is revealed in Duncan's published and unpublished works that he draws constantly upon his own life and experiences as subject matter. The autobiographies appear almost as a framework for the progression of his career, his achievements, failures and the discoveries of self, all of which are drawn upon for later evocation of both fact and feeling. Duncan's literary friendships, his marriage, his family, his farming and his love life are all faithfully recorded (albeit in such a way as to interest the reader), irrespective of the unflattering light in which he frequently appears.

In a diary[5] Duncan wrote: '*How to Make Enemies* appeared yesterday. I glanced at it, but didn't feel gratified: a series of anecdotes which fail to reveal me even to myself'. He later adds 'a review [in the *Times Literary Supplement*] points out that I must be one of the most unlikable persons alive'. And after the publication of *Obsessed* Duncan wrote in his Log Book:

> Mr Philip Zeigle (of Messrs Collins – publisher) who is reading the three volumes of autobiography with a view to a possible reprint, wrote to Eric Glass [agent] that he'd read *Obsessed* and thought it 'beautifully written' but revealed such an unpleasant and obnoxious personality, he would not publish anything of mine nor would he ever wish to meet me. [6]

Duncan comments, outraged, that '*Obsessed* does not reveal a moral nature, but not an obnoxious or sinister person'.[7]

Duncan may not have revealed himself to himself, but he does appear to have been at pains to present himself as extremely selfish. As Colin Wilson claims, this ability to deflate himself and use his own weaknesses and his real self in his works is Duncan's strength. Duncan himself found this self-flagellation acceptable in the sense that 'it is preferable to hang yourself than be beheaded with a bread knife.' He claimed to have written *Obsessed*

> in self-defence, believing it is preferable to attack oneself than be silent and thus encourage others to invent libels, or untruths which they peddle behind my back.

Duncan wants to admit all 'before well-subsidised and assiduous PhD's do more harm' than he did himself.[8] This reaffirms his comment (quoted in Chapter Two) that 'when the fox hangs himself he is at least saved from the hounds'.[9]

In an unedited manuscript of *Obsessed* Duncan explains that he chose the title *How to Make Enemies* 'not because my book is spiteful or indiscreet but because I have come to realise that my refusal during my life to conform or join any political or artistic groups has led to my having few friends or colleagues'.[10] Pound's label for Duncan as 'the lone wolf of English letters' is apt in this respect.

Duncan's first two autobiographies lost him several friends, including Pound and Eliot. In this same manuscript he confesses that he revealed more of Eliot than his friend wished. Eliot's obsession with privacy led him in his will to ban any biography. Duncan had revealed Eliot's 'fastidiousness', which Duncan feared had been interpreted as 'homosexuality' – towards which Eliot's attitude was un-balanced.

On reading the proofs of *How to Make Enemies* in his role as publisher, Eliot alerted Dorothy Pound's solicitors to Duncan's reference to Mary as Ezra's 'only' child, by his mistress Olga Rudge. According to Duncan, Ezra and Olga had wanted him to state publicly that this was the case, thus ignoring the existence of Pound's son, and casting doubt on the legitimacy of this male heir. To avoid a libel action, this reference had to be removed. Instead Duncan refers to Olga 'who was the mother of his [Pound's] daughter'. Neither Pound nor Eliot forgave him. Two more quarrels with Eliot, one of which (over a publishing matter) reached the High Court, compounded their disagreements. The other concerned Duncan's sale of some of Eliot's letters, concerning Ezra Pound, to Texas University.

Such misunderstandings,[11] although they are revealed and explained in private papers and in manuscripts for some 'assiduous PhD' to investigate, coupled with some unflattering anecdotes in the autobiographies, do expose a certain artistic spite. They reveal elements of an unpleasant personality, a lack of conventional morality and an overall selfishness. They also disclose Duncan's 'complexity as a human being'.[12] Wilson says that 'the key to some of this complexity is in these autobiographies'. Yet they are, as he also suggests, 'in the nature of a deliberate red herring', inasmuch as Duncan is a dramatist whose most interesting creation is himself'.[13] They describe the man, the source from which was released the vision within Duncan's mind.

His appetite for self-torture or punishment is especially apparent in *Obsessed*. This third volume of autobiography is concerned with Duncan's love for the actress Virginia Maskell, and was written after her marriage and tragically early death. Here Duncan exposes himself forcefully as a selfish man, as he has done time and time again. In his diary he writes:

How selfish grief is. How much do I mourn for Virginia, how much more for myself who died in her? We were one another. Let no prying eyes who read these pages conclude that this means I would not grieve as much for Rose-Marie. I loved both. You cannot measure love. Perhaps love is need? I don't know.

This continuous search, this questioning of self, life and feeling, is for Duncan an obsessive procedure. The passage continues:

> I have no urge towards any divinity. I wish to release
> the vision within my mind. To refine my love, to in-
> crease my sensitivity, awareness and consciousness. . . .
> That is my way – it seems to lead through hell
> > But the hell we accept
> > Is the only heaven we ever know.[14]

Whatever one thinks of such a man, self-confessed and self-obsessed, who put those he loved through that same hell in his disregard for their sensibilities, one can, in part, stand back and observe with some admiration such self-destructive honesty. Duncan acknowledges his inability to behave or feel differently in the lines:

> It is not that we are indifferent to their loss,
> but are completely deaf to their cry and unaware
> > of it.
> It is only when we are the losers
> that we gain, are given
> Awareness of what we've done to others
> then hope that they can forgive and we are ourselves
> > forgiven. [15]

In spite of the 'unlikable person' thus revealed in the autobiographies, Duncan retained the love and admiration of as many people as he lost, including, and uniquely, the wife and daughter who knew him best.

These three volumes of autobiography are the 'note-books' of Duncan's life. The favourite and characteristic phrases which recur frequently to haunt Duncan's poetry, plays and short stories are to be found here, too. He often uses the lines, 'It rained behind my eyes', 'slow eyes', 'we are dead when we cease to be children. Not all the dead are buried',[16] 'those who can be parted never loved'. Duncan's phraseology is full of imagery and humour, as in such lines as 'the house was full of your absence',[17] 'I eventually followed myself back to your room',[18] 'the next morning my impulse was to run from the house she had emptied of everything but her absence'.[19] Poetic prose startles from the page, as in a description of hotel rooms as 'not rooms but cells, where loneliness drips from the walls, silence screams from the ceiling, where the mean gas fire has a lascivious meter'.[20] Eliot, when discussing Duncan's 'immoral' play, *The Catalyst*, looked him 'straight in the leg'.[21] The prostitute in the poem 'Judas' knew 'which side her bed was buttered'.[22] As Zeigle noted, whatever his personal judgements on the author the autobiographies are 'beautifully written'.

Such biographical evidence supplied by the author is largely 'irrelevant in evaluating the writer's work', but as Duncan also said 'experiences do not describe an artist; an artist describes his experiences'.[23] All Duncan's work describes his experiences of life. Through his art he draws on that life to convey to the reader that which he has filtered, highlighted, embellished and learned from, in order to communicate his consciousness. Anecdotes are drawn upon for fictional plots. Poetic methods are revealed which are used in later articles on literature and education. The experiences of life in India with Gandhi, working in a coal mine, a Marxist experiment in farming, and of course love, both marital and extra-marital, are all themes of his work. They are the well of knowledge, or centre of consciousness, from which Duncan draws.

Although not wishing to appear as a 'mere gossip columnist on the Hills of Parnasses',[24] Duncan does, throughout his autobiographies and personal papers (and in the arrogance of his employing a secretary to request from his friends the return of his letters to them) appear to want academic or biographical investigation into his work. He is at pains to show that he is a catalyst in the unhappiness and lives of others. In his diary he says,

> Bless Rose-Marie and Briony for their sweet understanding. Rose-Marie watches me crying for another woman; and only love and concern comes from her. Let that paragraph for all times speak for her.[25]

Duncan's sketchbooks are littered with sketches of pelicans, entitled the 'melancholy melican'.[26] Rose-Marie says that the pelican will reputedly peck its own breast until it kills itself.[27] Perhaps Duncan, is the (me) pelican. However, this critic, in this context, 'cannot supplement [her] knowledge of external facts with psychological conjectures about inner experience',[28] which Eliot cites as a danger in biographical criticism.

4

A Prolific Writer of Great Diversity

The major areas of Duncan's literary concern are poetry, autobiography, drama – and a diverse and complex 'miscellanea' in which lies much of popular appeal. The range of this work includes the journalistic, the instructional, the appreciative and the fictional. A wide selection has been used here in order to suggest Duncan's multifarious capabilities and talents.

This 'lone wolf of English letters' earned his bread with both pen and spade, the satisfaction with one complementing the other. This is illustrated in Duncan's ability to combine the two in his distinctive style and language. His association with Lord Beaverbrook (formerly Max Aitken) led to Duncan's authorship of 'Jan's Journal', a regular Saturday feature in the London *Evening Standard*, of which volumes were collected as *Jan's Journal* [1] and *Jan at the Blue Fox*. [2] The former is dedicated to Beaverbrook, 'for it was he who suggested that I should write it and then gave me every encouragement while doing so'. In the foreword by Herbert Gunn [3] Jan is described as a poet as well as a peasant –

. . . not in the least an intellectual if you define that word as meaning someone who wears horn-rimmed spectacles and says 'whom'. He is a practical farmer, earthy, capable, with a strongly-developed instinctive understanding of birds and beasts and flowers and crops; and simultaneously he is a sensitive, cultivated artist with a sharp palate for most kinds of aesthetic pleasure. It is a magical combination.

Gunn goes on to describe *Jan's Journal* as 'a countryman's good humoured insight into human nature allied to an artist's imagination and an artist's feeling for words'.

These articles can stand alone as 'literature', anecdotal, amusing and written in captivating prose, exemplified by such lines as: 'the soil is still damp enough to slide from the plough, yet dry enough to crumble under the harrow'; 'the Spring has gushed from the earth like a fountain'; 'Yet in spite of Spring's generosity and the absurd affluence of it all, with the first wild flowers enlivening the bare hedge and the sense of promise even in the gorse, the only thing that smiles this Spring is the sun itself.' Of his promise to his wife to grow more interesting vegetables he writes: 'Like much on a farm, last year's promises get ploughed under this year's endeavour.'[4]

Yet biographical knowledge reveals many supposedly fictitious incidents to be true. A feature on tobacco growing is drawn from Duncan's *Journal of a Husbandman,*[5] the diary of his progress in farming, as confirmed by 'As if I had not enough distractions, tobacco became another; not content with smoking it to excess, I began to grow it.'[6] One could continue with lists of references to Duncan's own life which recur in his fiction to show the extent to which the man and his work are one. The cross references can become more complicated, as when Duncan writes in

Journal of a Husbandman. 'It is possible to write a sonnet or a canzone with hedgewood. A neighbour showed me how to do it.'[7] The same comparison is found in *All Men are Islands* and expanded upon some pages later with the lines: 'Hedging is the most satisfying of all farm jobs so long as the hook is sharp and the saw set; otherwise it is as exasperating as writing with a broom.'[8]

It is, so far, impossible to reach a conclusion as to why so many ideas, themes and actual lines are to be found so frequently and repetitively in Duncan's work. The man and his work often appear as mirror images, confirmed by biographical detail proffered by the man himself, by his friends and family, or in the works themselves. The repetition is probably not due to any lack of new material in the writer's life or imagination, or to any decline in his ability or vitality. Perhaps some ill-timed publishing is to blame, or maybe the obsession with 'self' of a writer who received limited attention during his career and was anxious to be heard. Possibly, it is just a revelation of his own artistic temperament. Haueter aptly sums up this elusiveness when he says that all Duncan's works 'are, as it were, like the loose pieces of a kaleidoscope. Each of them is a variation of a contribution to the underlying pattern.'[9]

Duncan is the Jan of *Jan at the Blue Fox*, about which the magazine *Cheshire Life* commented: 'There is humour, a tolerance of human weakness and much wisdom'[10] — some of Duncan's own qualities. The authorial voice is heard in the lines: 'And what does it matter whether my facts are correct so long as my lies are true? And what harm is there in being able to see the rose on the tree you forgot to plant?'[11]

Home Made Home [12] is not a textbook. Duncan said it 'began as a letter to some soldier unknown to me who wrote from Libya asking whether I could suggest any way he could find a home in the country after the war.'[13] Duncan is, in this book, 'concerned with a homestead which, on three acres, will provide a degree of subsistence'.[14] It is a book of suggestions about farming, building, prices and materials, but written with the philosophical profundity and wit typified by such lines as 'Decoration is no more a matter of paint than clothes are of wool'; 'the chief virtue of a fashion is that it changes'; 'the family is the beginning of responsibility and responsibility is the beginning of society'.[15]

Duncan edited a periodical, *The Townsman*, which began as a literary quarterly and expanded to include articles on farming. Appropriately, Duncan describes literature as 'the proper husbanding of words'.[16] Diversely he was a film and dramatic critic (which is explored in Chapter Five). Other diffused works include those already mentioned on Dante and Rochester, *Gandhi: Selected Writings* [17] and *Working with Britten: a Personal Memoir.* [18] The latter, in which Duncan confirms his views on biographical matters with 'I do not think that facts or opinions about an artist's life are necessary to the appreciation of his work', [19] also tells of his joint venture with Britten, *The Rape of Lucretia* in 1946 (the libretto being by Duncan), and of *Amo Ergo Sum*, a wedding anthem for which Duncan wrote the words in 1949. This musical involvement illustrates the extent of the artist's versatility.

During the last five years of Duncan's life he was involved in the compilation of several collections of opinions on various subjects. They are reminiscent of the Victorian gift book, inasmuch as they are not the work of the dedicated artist and lack the 'soul' of the author. The *Encyclopaedia of Ignorance* [20] is the product of scientists invited to state what they would most like to know; only the Preface bears the stamp of Duncan, with 'Compared to the pond of knowledge, our ignorance remains atlantic.' *The Encyclopaedia of Medical Ignorance* [21] is on similar lines, focusing on the 'ignorance of how our own bodies and minds function in health and disease'.

Lying Truths is a critical scrutiny of current beliefs and conventions, its Introduction stating that 'whereas the media spread ideas, it is the purpose of this book to disrupt them'. Duncan's contribution, on the assumption that merit is always recognised, is more in keeping with his previous literary views:

> My target is the current and persistent notion that merit is inevitably, eventually recognised. This absurd belief is generally applied to creative work in the arts or sciences. . . . It removes any burden from the social conscience for failing to recognise and removes from people any guilt for their inability to distinguish between taste and fashion.

Duncan lists those passed by — Stravinsky, Hopkins (except by accident), Isaac Rosenberg (still hardly known in spite of Leavis's comments), and Survage, who shared a studio with Picasso ('almost totally unknown because he lacked his colleague's gift for self publicity . . . the better painter, not draughtsman'). Such a tragedy, he claims, is decreed by fashion and has little to do with the artist's work. He continues:

> Mob education and mass media which lower stan-
> dards and criteria perceptibly every decade only get
> the known names more widely known. We equate
> fashion with taste. . . . To assume merit is the
> assumption that we have perceptive critics, or to
> give them their correct title, journalists. [22]

This is a hobby-horse of Duncan's taken up in his autobiography [23] — but also linked with his own experiences in
the field of drama, as are discussed in the next chapter.

However, the subject of Duncan's attitude to the critics
leads conveniently into the next 'gift' book, published after
his death on 3 June 1982 and entitled *Critics' Gaffes*. It is
an amusing 'collection of best and funniest mistakes made
by critics of every land'. For example:

> To ascertain the merit of a poem is one thing; to
> determine the powers of the poet is another; the
> present paper aims at the latter. Such being the case,
> the faults of Keats's poetry may be divided into two
> classes: 1, those of youth and inexperience; 2, those
> of deficiency of genius. Out of the former he might
> (had his life been spared) have grown: the latter he
> would have kept till his death bed. [24]

Of the Impressionist School — 'a period of ignorance and
frenzy';[25] and of Edison's electric light — 'do not bother to
sell your gas shares. The electric light has no future.'[26]

Marx Refuted,[27] also published posthumously, is similarly compiled. Duncan's practical involvement in collective farming, his support for the Welsh miners in 1930 and his attitude to non-violence in industrial disputes, is retold in his contribution. Like the other volumes, this collection of essays and interviews sports impressive contributors, here including Bernard Levin, A. L. Rowse and Margaret Thatcher, to name but three. To extend the definition of the word 'work' (as applied to Duncan's literary output hitherto) from writer, to compiler and editor, is to reflect and confirm interests which are to be found throughout his artistic career.

Duncan made numerous contributions to collections of short stories concerning the supernatural, Cornwall, adultery and love. His contribution to *My Cornwall*[28] is a transcription from *All Men are Islands* of a beachcombing story of the retrieving of a barrel of burgundy.[29] Yet he concludes this piece with a typical poetic enquiry:

> The worst carpenter can find something there
> [in North Cornwall or Devon] he is capable of
> repairing, and the laziest gardener soon sees signs of
> order where there was chaos and weeds before. Was
> that also my reason? I do not know. As usual, there
> is nothing for it but to write on, in order to discover
> what one knows but does not realise.

This is another indication, found in an unlikely place, of how involved Duncan the man was with Duncan the writer.

Two of the notions which appealed to Duncan were 'obtaining something for nothing' and the dead haunting the living. He combines these in several short stories published in other and his own collections, such as 'The Diary of a Poltergeist',[30] 'Consanguinity',[31] and 'When we Dead Awaken'.[32] To return to the possible reasons for Duncan's repetition of so much of his material, perhaps the appeal of the notion of 'obtaining something for nothing' was part of this plurality of publication – a return on very little effort!

Perhaps the short story writer needs to be especially gifted, lacking as he does the scope of the full-length novelist to expand, manoeuvre, develop or play with his tale. His story must be succinct and must hold the reader's attention from the first. One is prepared to 'get into' a novel, but a short story can all too easily be put aside in order to progress to the next. Duncan was a superb short storyteller, using language of the 'maximum charge'. His style lends itself to this art, successfully combining the ingredients of wit, alertness, spice and spite. As a man he also embodied these qualities, and his experience of life is the clay to which he applied his tools.

The Perfect Mistress,[33] according to *The Times*, was 'a very pretty light bunch of viper's bugloss and enchanter's nightshade', which established the author as a 'master story teller'.[34] Duncan's views are embodied in his fiction as in his life. *The Last Adam*, amongst others, illustrates especially his scathing views about literature in such lines as 'I realised that the only essential to the form of the English novel is that it should have two covers', and in his reference to 'the Dead Sea of Criticism'.[35]

Time and space do not permit even a list of the connections between the life of Duncan and that which is portrayed in his short stories. However, *Mr and Mrs Mouse* must be an exception.[36] This was Duncan's first fairy story, described on its dust jacket as a 'literary primrose which needs no explanation or justification . . . the poet now finds the fairy story an important vehicle'. The fairy story is defined on the cover of *Tale of Tails* [37] as that 'written for children between the ages of ten and one hundred'. Whilst requiring no 'explanation or justification', this particularly touching tale is especially pertinent to my argument that biographical knowledge of the author adds to the appreciation of his work.

Mr and Mrs. Mouse is dedicated to Rose-Marie: 'I wrote this little piece for you in the back of a car while being driven from Nairobi down to Mombasa. If you like it, I'll write some more fairy tales.' The story, so recognisable as Duncan's work, captures the relationship between Duncan and his wife and 'their dependence on one another'.[38] Of himself, Mr Mouse, 'many admired his voice; all were impressed by his international reputation' (Duncan's plays were very popular in Germany), and he always 'scampered back to Mrs Mouse' after his affairs. 'She used to tell herself and close friends that he was an unfaithful philanderer who was really not worth loving. However, nobody was fooled by this, including Mrs Mouse herself, who tried so hard to bandage this wound that love is.'

Mr Mouse 'was not a brave man', who with his fear of loneliness dared to look at the desert his life would become if anything happened to Mrs Mouse. 'It was loneliness that was destroying me as it always had done. I realised now for the first time that the only real cure for loneliness is to find myself.'[39] 'All she could think of was that Mr Mouse who had a weak chest would probably die first'. A (fictitious) attempt to die together fails as 'again a wave flung them as flotsam and left them as jetsam, among the pebbles'.

The beach is suggestive of Welcombe; their 'little burrow in the hedge of the field' and the boiling of kettles on 'a few bits of dried gorse in the embers' of their life together at West Mill. Duncan's love of Schubert is portrayed as Mr Mouse rehearses some Schubert songs for a recital he planned to give in Canada during the summer. (Their son, Roger, was living in Canada at the time.)

Duncan's selfishness is manifested when Mrs Mouse is diagnosed by Dr Badger as suffering from bronchitis. His 'what shall I do without her?' is reminiscent of the situation in which Rose-Marie haemorrhaged with tuberculosis at West Mill.[40] Badger says, 'You must think of your wife now and look after her. It is she who is ill, though with care she'll pull through all right.' Rose-Marie's real-life doctor had been critical of Duncan's failure to notice his wife's enormous weight loss and obvious illness. Duncan's self-confessed reaction was to wake her up, as 'I needed her sympathy'. As he took over her nursing he observed, 'There was no sacrifice I would not make for myself, I knew I could not bear my own life without her. When another person's life reminds us of how vulnerable and precious is our own, it is as near to love as most of us ever get.'[41]. This is his tribute to Rose-Marie.

The ending is sad. Mr Mouse drops dead of a heart attack, shocked at the thought of 'no Mrs Mouse', since 'imagination is a more serious disease than bronchitis'. It is ironic that Duncan died of lung cancer, which was initially diagnosed as bronchitis, reconciled to and living with

Rose-Marie at Home Farm. Although his wife did not literally jump 'down into the grave and lay herself down beside him', some of her died too. The final line of the story is a beautiful tribute to a real-life story of sorrow and joy – 'Then all the birds plucked feathers from their own breasts with their beaks and the night itself cried with all its stars.'[42]

The range, versatility and prolific extent of the work of this talented writer illustrate how integral a part his work played in his life. The area of his dramatic writing is explored in the final chapter. According to Rose-Marie, Duncan was a compulsive writer, needing to practice his art every day of his life with her. Much of Duncan's work in those fields hitherto explored remains unpublished, just as his vital contribution to the English Stage Company, examined in Chapter Five, remains largely unrecognised.

Illustrations

1. Ronald Duncan as a youth, *c.* 1932.

2. Ronald's mother ('Mole'), as a young woman.

3. Duncan's future wife, Rose Marie Hansom, in her early twenties.

4. West Mill at Welcombe Mouth, Devon – Rose Marie and Ronald Duncan's home from 1937.

5. Ronald Duncan with his daughter Briony at West Mill, *c.* 1941.

6. Signed photograph from Benjamin Britten of the composer and Peter Pears at work.

7. Ronald and Rose Marie with Benjamin Britten's sisters before a performance of *The Rape of Lucretia* (1946).

8. Scene from *The Rape of Lucretia*. Photo: Angus McBean, copyright Harvard Theatre Collection, supplied by courtesy of Britten-Pears Library, Aldeburgh.

9. Poster for Duncan's poetic drama, *This Way to the Tomb!* (1945).

10. Virginia Maskell as Cleone in Duncan's *The Catalyst* (1958). Photo: Houston Rogers.

11. Briony Duncan with Colin Wilson, early 1960s.

12. Scene from 1960 revival of *This Way to the Tomb!* Photo: Angus McBean, copyright Harvard Theatre Collection.

1. Ronald Duncan as a youth: possibly 1932, aged eighteen, taken at the time of or after his African trip in 1931.

2. Opposite page, top: Ronald's mother ('Mole'), Ethel Dunkelsbühler, *née* Canon, as a young woman, probably close to the time of her marriage to the writer's father, Reginald John, in 1913.

3. Opposite page, bottom: Rose Marie Hansom as a young woman – possibly in her early twenties, 1935 to 1937, before or at the time of meeting her future husband, Ronald.

4. Above: West Mill at Welcombe Mouth, North Devon, where Rose Marie and Ronald Duncan set up home in late 1937. This was where the Duncan family and their friends would gather to farm, fish, write, compose and paint, until near the time of Ronald's death in 1982.

5. Left: Ronald with his daughter Briony at West Mill, *circa* 1941.

6. Below: a signed photograph from Benjamin Britten of the composer and Peter Pears at work. Both were frequent visitors to Devon, especially during the nineteen forties and 'fifties, Duncan and Britten's busiest collaborative period.

Rose Marie –
with much love
P.....
Ben !

7. Ronald and Rose Marie with Benjamin Britten's sisters at Glyndebourne before a 1946 performance of *The Rape of Lucretia*, for which Duncan wrote the libretto.

8. Right to left: Margaret Ritchie (Lucia), Kathleen Ferrier (Lucretia), and Anna Pollak (Bianca) in Act I, Scene ii of *The Rape of Lucretia* at Glyndebourne Opera House, Sussex, in June, 1946.
Photo: Angus McBean.

MERCURY THEATRE

IN REPERTORY

1	2
This way to the tomb!	**The shadow factory**
DUNCAN · BRITTEN	ANNE RIDLER

The Pilgrim Players in association with the Arts Council of Great Britain

ROBERT SPEAIGHT · **ALAN WHEATLEY**

BOTH PLAYS PRODUCED BY E. MARTIN BROWNE

NIGHTLY AT 7 · MATINEES THURSDAY AND SATURDAY 2.30

for dates and times apply Box Office (Park 5700)

NOTTING HILL GATE W·11

TUBE : Central Line   BUSES : 12, 17, 27, 28, 31, 52, 88   METRO : Inner Circle

9. Left: poster for Duncan's poetic drama, *This Way to the Tomb!* first performed by E. Martin Browne's Pilgrim Players in 1945 at the Mercury Theatre, London.

10. Bottom left: Virginia Maskell as Cleone in the playwright's controversial drama *The Catalyst*, produced at the Arts, March 1958. Photo: Houston Rogers.

11. Bottom right: Briony Duncan with the writer Colin Wilson, a close friend of her father's, early 1960s.

12. A scene from the 1960 revival of *This Way to the Tomb!* at the Arts Theatre, London. Left to right: Dawn Brooks (Lechery), Iain Cuthbertson (St Anthony), and Roland Curram (Gluttony). Photo: Angus McBean.

5

Drama and Criticism

Duncan's comments that 'We equate fashion with taste' and that 'To assume merit is the assumption that we have perceptive critics, or to give them their correct title, journalists' are referred to in Chapter Four. From this and other unflattering comments, it is clear that critics ranked low in Duncan's estimation. Such an attitude can easily be dismissed as the 'sour grapes' of a less celebrated artist who suffered, often severely, at the hands of the critics. However, Duncan was employed as a film and a dramatic critic himself, and therefore had experience of criticism at source and reception. Current fashion, of which he was scathing, played as large a part as did cruel criticism in the bitterness he felt later in his career.

Of the role of film critic, Duncan said 'it was a terrible chore. No wonder critics are moronic: their routine would reduce anybody to idiocy.' He saw two, sometimes three, films a day, was duly wooed with alcohol and by hostesses on behalf of American companies for his good opinion. In reaction, his 'criticism became increasingly violent'.[1]

'The lowest I have sunk, so far in my life', Duncan claimed, 'was when I became a dramatic critic.' This he felt it his duty to do – as a stand-in for Beverley Baxter[2] – because he 'had maintained that poetry could only be criticised by poets, music by composers and drama by dramatists',[3] echoing the strong feelings of his friend and mentor Ezra Pound. 'Having had five or six of my own plays staged in the West End', he felt especially suited to the job.

> I knew of some of the difficulties, the compromises, the playwright agrees to under pressure; the limitations placed on the producer under duress of the management; the restrictions placed on the actor's performance to please either the producer, the management or the dramatist. [4]

Duncan failed in the role. He was disgusted by his first article, which he destroyed, because it was so 'savage and uncompromising' that it would probably have closed the play. Having suffered 'too many cruel criticisms' himself, he felt that a judge had to be indifferent. This attitude resulted in dull reviews. Beaverbrook said to him, 'I wanted you to write a bright piece, I'm not interested in justice, but good journalism. A good critic has to attack, attack, attack.' [5] Justice and merit, it would appear, had no place in the savage world of 'commercial' art. Duncan never came to terms with this situation.

This Way to the Tomb, Duncan's most famous and successful play, ran for over a year at the Mercury Theatre in London. The criticism he received was varied. *The Stage* observed:

> The author in an extremely complex rhyming scheme never before achieved in English [Duncan's aim was to show that one could use poetry without seeming to use poetic language] ably presents the traditional

devotion of the age. His verse has soothing rhythm with intellectual appeal and a pleasant ripple of humour, but one must complain of overweight of words and a somewhat uneven treatment. [6]

The Weekly Review described the problem of poetic drama, so far as this play was concerned, as one of 'terrible obscurity like that which oppresses us in drama',[7] while *The Observer* claimed that: 'Mr Ronald Duncan's packed, cerebral speeches do not kindle a beacon in the heaven kissing hill, they are for study rather than stage'. [8] Yet even the kindest comments were perhaps to Duncan's detriment, as had been the tremendous success of the play. It was a prize too easily won. He said of himself, 'I was in fashion, but because that fashion was me, I mistook it for good taste.'[9] Edmund Blunden wrote to Duncan in these terms:

> my wife had at last obtained tickets, and we can now take our places in decent society as having direct knowledge of one of the finest dramatic 'idealisms' (Shelley has used the right word) of these times. [10]

The most flattering review was written by Beverley Baxter:

> What manner of man is this Cornwall's farmer who can mix a Bach Chorale and American Jazz and make it a coherent whole? The beauty of St. Anthony's ruminations was the more compelling because the author never gave the impression of striving for fine writing. Who would not be stirred by such words as 'Christ lies in my heart like a fresh leaf in an old

book', 'loneliness is the wilderness of the soul'. One feels that the author has sat at the feet of Milton and of Shelley, strange tutors to a genius. But so skilfully does he invoke the magic of language that when temptation appears in the form of a woman it is asking too much of an actress to compete with the voluptuousness of words. What is the use of saying that this is an uneven piece of work? So is life. If we live in an age dominated by Calvary and the Atomic Bomb, why should a poet try to force his thoughts into a straitjacket? [11]

As a result of this play Duncan was labelled a religious poet, a view which he strongly contested. Feeling that the theatre had been truncated into religious plays, social plays, thrillers and so forth, he said: 'It nauseated me, too, to be called a religious poet. If *religio* meant 'to connect' how could any poet not be religious? How . . . can a meaningful play not have a religious connotation and a social implication too?' [12]

John Reid claimed that Duncan 'was Gnostic; the body imprisoned in the soul; nature evil; spirit good; evil with as much right to be as good . . . but Christ fascinated him, as with Graham Greene he found material there – for drama'. [13] This could be true. Duncan's body did imprison his soul in the same way as his talent enslaved the man.

According to E. W. F. Tomlin, 'Duncan seems to have arrived at the conclusion that life is empty and liable to degradation without at least some sort of natural religion.' [14] What this element contributes to the beauty of his work is a reverent but natural respect and appreciation for all that can be absorbed into the consciousness and into the being, whether good or bad.

Hinchcliffe describes *This Way to the Tomb* as a rare commercial success in comparison with the fortunes of plays by poets such as Norman Nicholson and Anne Ridler.

> Religious drama in verse is restricted in every sense, but it was part of that larger yearning to escape the merely social, moral and physical. The poets [at this time] began to reconsider the possibility of both language and the theatre; they provided roles in plays which trained actors and audiences, teaching the latter to listen and to listen seriously. [15]

In common with Eliot and Cocteau, Duncan disliked the realistic plays of the nineteenth century, which wanted a 'wider sense of theatre. . . . Suggesting that theatre was a place where serious matters happened and could be discussed [was] more important than their relative merits.' [16] Ironically, because of the effect of verse drama upon the audience's awareness of language as distinct from the visual, the way was paved for Beckett, Pinter, Wesker and for the kind of 'kitchen-sink', politically-biased drama which Duncan detested. To Wahl he said:

> I am not trying to make the drama realistic; I do not want drama to be life-like. I've said this again and again, and I've tried and tried to make drama bigger than life. So that we grow a little through it . . .
> I want to articulate or try to articulate the meanings behind things and make articulate what is not

articulate. . . . The theatre of naturalism . . . is
reducing the theatre to the boredom of life. [17]

Haueter claims that Duncan's plays were not written for
mass audiences, 'but for those who are ready to probe
deeper levels of consciousness together with the playwright'.[18] However, the day of the mass audience, the
theatre as a big commercial business, had arrived. Plays of
the social and realistic kind were in vogue. Duncan swiftly
became out of fashion.

This chapter is not directed wholly at attempting to
convince the reader that Duncan's plays reflect his life.
Duncan's once-considerable popularity must be stressed in
order to acknowledge and pay tribute to his contribution
to English drama. A better appreciation and understanding
of this is to be obtained by exploring the biographical.

Two examples perhaps will suffice to reinforce my earlier
arguments concerning the connections between Duncan's
drama and his life. Firstly, of *The Catalyst*, Duncan's best
and most serious play of the dozen or so he wrote, Virginia
Maskell said: 'I played your bloody life on stage, I'm
damned if I'm going to live it too.' [19] Secondly, of *St Spiv*
Duncan himself said: 'Critics and literary detectives have
sometimes speculated whether or not some part of my
plays had an autobiographical source. But none have sus-
pected that I took the final curtain of *St Spiv* straight from
my own experience.' [20] Duncan unavoidably spent a night
in a telephone kiosk and arranged an alarm call with the
operator (at a time when he had two plays running in
London), and commented that he was 'down but not yet
out'. Horace suffers the same fate in the play, and Lazarus

as he passes the phone box changes the 'Not Working' sign to 'Down and Out'. [21]

As a mere 'gossip columnist on the Hills of Parnassus', it is of interest that Deborah Kerr wrote to Duncan refusing the lead role in *The Catalyst* out of 'moral timidity' as she did not 'really like women loving other women . . . despite the fact that the husband and wife relationship and the husband-secretary relationship have some marvellous things to say – pertinent as well as amusing'. [22]

Such biographical information illuminates Duncan's then-current popularity, justifying to some extent his later bitterness. Colin Wilson defends Duncan's later behaviour by suggesting that 'Duncan's rise to fame was as abrupt as Byron's, and his subsequent repudiation by the critics was equally traumatic. Under the circumstances, it is not surprising that both Byron and Duncan developed a penchant for satire and a talent for making enemies.' [23]

The plays written by Duncan are largely taken from his own life and experiences. As Haueter says:

> His work is a work of relentless disclosure of the
> nature of man. Honesty is the basic condition;
> humility the way. This deadly serious honesty is
> perhaps what may shock many people acquainted
> with his work. They think it is immoral. [24]

This 'relentless disclosure' of the nature of man, because it is taken from his own experiences, is not only honest but undeniably brave.

Biographical knowledge can be used not only to help explain the bitterness which haunts some of Duncan's later works, but also to pay tribute to the author as the founder of the English Stage Company. This was Duncan's most lasting achievement — a by-product of his talent for persuading people to part with 'contributions', whether of their opinions (as seen in his 'compilation' books) or their cash. The Royal Court

> changed the life and work of many established artists
> by giving them opportunities for new directions and
> fresh growth. It has a widespread influence, still
> reverberating, upon attitudes to the theatre as an
> art, a trade and a social activity.[25]

Two months before his death, Duncan was seeking to correct allegations made by Richard Findlater, in his book on the history of the Company, which he considered to be defamation of character — contesting a reference to his 'rightish, high church ideals' and the claim that he 'founded the theatre in order to produce [his] own plays'.[26]

The conception and birth of the English Stage Company is described at length in *How to Make Enemies*. Its success, and Duncan's later dissatisfaction, must be the concern of a future biographer. Yet the original aims — to present new plays without bias towards any political or religious doctrine, neither excluding the realistic play nor the more imaginative drama; to achieve some stylisation in both acting and décor; to react against the box-set and the materialistic décor which made production so expensive that management could not afford to risk experimental plays — were largely achieved. That is rightly attributable in part to Duncan.

The venture, in Duncan's opinion, declined into 'a theatre which produces an opportunity for a clique . . . a different thing from a theatre which is actively creative. We have made a revolution in fashion which is a different thing from a revolution in taste.'[27]

The dialogue becomes very involved and embittered from this point in Duncan's personal correspondence, resulting in his resignation from the Company.[28] The point that needs stressing here is that whatever the controversial circumstances, yet to be fully investigated, Duncan's early achievements in this field should not be forgotten or underestimated. His commitment to the furtherance of the English theatre is clear, and such work is part and parcel of Duncan's literary whole.

In conclusion, and as anticipated in my personal introduction, experience of life, especially reflected in poetry, is both pleasure and pain almost too personal to be shared even between pen and paper. Duncan shares his path of discovery through life with his readers. His life is his work and his work is his life, as seen through the eyes of the gifted artist. His work adds to the understanding of the man, and biographical knowledge of the man contributes to the understanding and greater appreciation of his work, and indeed of much of life itself. But let the man claiming the role of the Bard speak finally for himself:

I had discovered that I was a poet, and to be a poet is not just a concern with words; it is to bleed when you are not wounded: it is to be wounded when you are not hit: it is to enjoy so intensely that enjoyment is unbearable, another kind of pain. The decision to be an artist is not merely the decision to apply yourself to paint, to notes or to words. It is the decision to be conscious and that is to suffer something like the pains of birth with every moment. It is to be born daily, to die hourly.

The essence of an artist is his internal vision, not his technical skill; many craftsmen acquire that. A vision may be an act of grace, but that grace is heavy, an intolerable burden. . . . You feel that you have denied yourself, betrayed yourself and crucified yourself, not gloriously but ridiculously. [29]

Appendixes

Appendix i

Notes for a Planned Book on English Literature

I do not regard poetry as decoration, as embroidery, as a pretty trifle recollected in idleness for idleness.

The poet's own personality, his own psychic difficulties or amorous entanglements are, in the last analysis, frivolous and trivial.

But to-day Personality is at a premium. Even the most serious scholars in lit. find themselves mere gossip columnists on the Hills of Parnassus.

And we have reached that point where the life of a poet is more important than his poetry.

I believe that a poem is a communication, not a decoration, an urgent communication and not a casual postcard on the back of a pretty view.

I use the word communication advisedly, a moment of communion (the centre of religious experience of spiritual growth).

And a poem is a point of growth within our consciousness.

What he is communicating is the prime factor.

The poem, the thing expressed, must be lucid, it must cohere.

Judged good or bad, first by the content, the thing said, and secondly by the effectiveness of the statement.

The value of being is in the consciousness.

The world is dark, poetry is the light in it.

Art and poetry must be about something, convey something, and can be judged firstly by the content, the value of its statement and secondly, the effectiveness with which it says it. This is the keel of criticism and criticism deserves to sink if it is without these two criteria.

The Ronald Duncan Papers: the New Collection

Appendix ii

From a Scrapbook of Press Cuttings.

Duncan often described, similarly to Clare, as a Cornish
farmer, problem of poetic drama 'terrible obscurity like
that which oppresses us in dreams'.

Weekly Review, 18 Oct. 1945

The author in an extremely complex rhyming-scheme,
never before achieved in English, ably presents the
traditional devotion of the age. His verse has soothing
rhythm with intellectual appeal, and a pleasant ripple of
humour, but one must complain of overweight of words
and a somewhat uneven treatment.

Stage, 18 Oct. 1945

The verse is strongly knit, supple and sonorous.

The Guardian, 19 Oct. 1945

This Way to the Tomb. RD emerges from the ordeal of
playwright for the stage a more promising figure than that
of Thornton Wilder, although there is a little too slavish
a following after Eliot and Auden.

Catholic Herald, 26 Oct. 1945

What manner of man is this Cornwall's farmer who can
mix a Bach Chorale and American Jazz and make it a

coherent whole? The beauty of St. Anthony's ruminations was the more compelling because the author never gave the impression of striving for fine writing. Who would not be stirred by such words as 'Christ lies in my heart like a fresh leaf in an old book', 'loneliness is the wilderness of the soul'. One feels that the author has sat at the feet of Milton and of Shelley, strange tutors to genius. But so skilfully does he invoke the magic of language that when temptation appears in the form of a woman is it asking too much of an actress to compete with the voluptuousness of words? What is the use of saying as some critics have done that this is an uneven piece of work? So is life. If we live in an age dominated by Calvary and the Atomic Bomb, why should a poet try to force his thoughts into a straitjacket?

Beverley Baxter, *Evening Standard*, 3 Nov. 1945

Appendix iii

English with Tears

It would be interesting to know how many people
take the English Tripos because they intend to become
writers. Although most of them end as schoolmasters
or degenerate into Arts Council bureaucrats, that was
not their original ambition. Their failure is not all
their own, but is due to the inability of the English
Faculty to train a person to earn his living with
his pen.

It is questionable whether the Faculty discharges its
responsibilities of teaching the undergraduate how to
read. It is certain that it never attempts the problem
of how to write.

When I went up to the University, I had already
decided that I would devote myself to writing poetry,
but even with this intention I found that after three years
of reading English I had little knowledge of any literary
form or of the technicalities of poetry. My notebooks
from the lectures are littered with irrelevant dates of
the poets' lives, but nobody thought it worth while to
instruct us how to make a canzone, or even inform us
about the intricacies of the sestina or sonnet. Many
who get a first in the Tripos could not answer the most
elementary questions on prosody or metrics. Biographical
details clutter their predatory minds.

As it now stands, the English Tripos at any University
is a mere banal extension of the School Certificate; the
collection of facts rather than the refining of sensibility;
the grading of poets rather than the knowledge of form.
Most of the supervisions are spent in the ridiculous
parlour game of 'spot the quotation', or in that pastime
borrowed from the detective thriller, 'guess the influence',
and in proving that everybody is derivative from somebody. Which mild donnish hobby has little to do with
how to write or how to read.

Compare the dilemma of a person who wishes to
become a writer, and reads the English Tripos, with
somebody who intends to become a doctor, an architect
or even a musician. It is fair to say that the medical
student gathers more than the dates of Hervey's life.
He gets his nose into a hospital. Similarly, the School
of Architecture is not wholly concerned with the lives
of Vanbrugh and Wren. A T-square and drawing board
are somewhere on the horizon, though it is regrettable
that the School does not teach how to mix cement or
set a lintel. And even a musician learns the range of his
instruments, acquires some idea of counterpoint and
tries his hand at one or two exercises in composition.
Which efforts cannot in any way detract from his
appreciation of Vivaldi.

The quickest way to understand a form is to try to
work within it.

I am not suggesting that the humanities should be
abandoned. I am *not* suggesting that the English Faculty
should be turned into an extension of Lime Grove Studios
or that Mr Hugh Beaumont should be given the Chair.

It is perhaps bad enough that the sciences should be tethered to industry. But I do believe that the syllabus should be revised and a few lectures given to those people to have such respect for literature that they intend to earn their living by keeping it alive. And it is not too much to suggest that one or two lectures might usefully be given by people who have succeeded in doing this.

Nor need this approach detract from the ordinary academic appreciation of the classics. It is quite obvious that the best of Shakespeare can only be assessed if it is realised that it was written to be played. A lecture by Michael Redgrave, for instance, on *Macbeth* could teach us more about the flexibility of the verse in that play than all the 'Seven Types of Ambiguity' and Mr Dover Wilson rolled together.

Obviously, a theatre should be the laboratory for the English Faculty, as the Mond is for Physics.

I was recently asked to be one of the three adjudicators for a University play competition. I took my task seriously, and read over 20 well typed scripts. We came to the decision that not one of the plays was actable or deserved production. The authors had obviously worked hard. Many of them had literary talent. It is a pity that such efforts should end in frustration, lacking the knowledge of the ABC of dramatic construction. Is dramatic construction nothing to do with the English Tripos? Is it possible to appreciate Shakespeare without some knowledge of it? It is no use fobbing off the contemporary student with Aristotle's unities. Or, if they are considered of value, why not go further?

In prose the situation is no better. A study of Jane Austen, George Eliot and the Brontë sisters has yet to produce any appreciation of the novel as a form *per se*. It is more than a certain number of works bound together by two covers. Stylistic questions such as the balance of direct reporting with the author's asides are matters not touched upon. Lawrence's clumsiness in this respect still goes unnoticed.

The graduate sets off to Fleet Street without even the most elementary knowledge of the art of paraphrase, précis or concision, and as little qualified for journalism as he is for belles lettres. Many editors have complained to me that they find an elementary schoolboy easier to train than a graduate from the universities — and this is not wholly an adverse comment on the quality of journalism. People leave the universities believing that metaphor and imagery are all of style, and without any training in lucidity or concision. A glance at *The Times* leaders proves this point. It would be interesting to know what percentages are given, when the English Tripos papers are marked, to the accuracy of biographical facts, and to the candidate's prose style.

It may well be that no revision of the English syllabus could meet the case, and that a person who wishes to earn his living as a writer would do better to apprentice himself to a practising writer. Even a novelist without any great literary pretensions can teach more of the craft of writing than the most erudite critic. If I have any knowledge of that craft myself, I owe it more to Ezra Pound's blue pencil and to Eliot's comments and queries in the margin than to the lectures of Mrs Bennett or Dr Tillyard.

It might be argued that such apprenticeship should follow the academic course as it now stands. But the fact is that very few people have an independent income to enable them to devote themselves to literature, and consequently they have to be able to earn their living at it as soon as they leave the University; or they are inevitably swallowed up by those enormous bureaucratic institutions which live like parasites on the periphery.

As things are now, the graduate is unlikely to be able to earn a penny in journalism, television or the theatre before he is 32. Very few indeed can stand it that long. And perhaps this is one of the reasons why today there are so few writers of promise.

Appendix iv

Dante the Maker

by William Anderson

(*Routledge and Kegan Paul, £18.00*)

Here we are again: another book about a poet, 500 pages
at £18.00, while the poet himself goes unread and is out
of print. But what does that matter? Scholars need
subjects and PhDs breed PhDs. And Mr Anderson has
been a most assiduous mole; he has burrowed hard,
worked hard, as his bibliography proves, but it is all
academia; no poetry surfaces.

When was Dante's *Vita Nuova* last published? As for
De Vulgari Eloquentia — I should know, because I have just
sent it to be published myself and will pay for it out of
my own pocket (having had an application for a grant
turned down by the South East Arts Association). No
matter, we are a literate nation and so long as we have
books about poets, there is no need to read the sods
themselves. Cui bono? Scholarship.

If this book encouraged anybody to road Dante
I would approve it. But it won't. Its purpose is to give
the 'student' a background, which is not a spine. Instead
of the publication of this book, about it and about, how
many paper backs of *The Divine Comedy* could have been
printed? My guess is that there are not twenty people in
this country who have read the poem — though of course

everybody approves it. To misquote the last line of the
Dunciad: 'Universal scholarship covers all.'

I notice that Mr Anderson at least nods in Guido
Cavalcanti's direction and refers to *Donna Mi Pregha*. But
he fails to comment that Dante regarded Cavalcanti as his
master; nor does he refer to Ezra Pound's excellent book
on Cavalcanti.

It is irrelevant to me, but perhaps of some interest
to scholars, that about twenty years ago the Persian
Ambassador in London told me that Dante had based
The Divine Comedy on a Persian poem. He offered me a
house in Persia and a housekeeper of the right dimen-
sions, if I would go out there to look at the Persian
text. But I am no scholar and am not interested in roots,
but fruits.

As to Mr Anderson's occasional quotations from
The Divine Comedy, he omits to tell us whose translation
he is using. They are all poor. I suppose Laurence
Binyon's is the best. I remember telling T. S. Eliot one
day that Dorothy Sayers had embarked on a new version,
to which his reply was: 'Better she got on with her
knitting.'

I say Binyon is the best. Better check that:

> *Per correr migliori acque alza le vele*
> *omai la navicella del mio ingegno,*
> *che lascia dietro a se mar si crudele;*
> *e cantero di quel secondo regno*
> *dove l'umano spirito si purga*
> *e di salire al ciel diventa degno.*
>
> (Canto I)

Binyon renders the above:

> *Now hoisteth sail the pinnace of my wit*
> > *For better waters, and more smoothly flies*
> > *Since of a sea so cruel she is quit,*
> *And of that second realm, which purifies*
> > *Man's spirit of its soilure, will I sing,*
> > *Where it becometh worthy of Paradise.*

Pound is wrong, I see. Binyon's version too is full of inversion. What do I mean? I mean surely it should run something like this, to improvise:

> *May the boisterous wind billow my slack mind,*
> > *Lift my frail craft from these rough waters*
> > *Where despair drowns, and elsewhere some hope find waters,*
> *Even briefly, though I know nothing alters,*
> > *Improves or changes human nature:*
> > *Like colts we're tethered, invisible our halters.*
> *May poetry long silenced have this future:*
> > *To be articulate and lucid once again.*

It is unfair to quote an author out of context, but what else can a reviewer do? Here is a fair example of Mr Anderson's. 'Earlier I suggested that there might be a relationship between the four levels of meaning in the interpretation of scripture and the levels of reality described in the Neoplatonic and cabalistic traditions. In Neoplatonic terms these would relate the One to the anagogic level, the Nous or Mind to the moral level, the World Soul to the allegorical level, and the spheres of creation to the literal level, and in Chapter 19 it was demonstrated how these levels could be seen in connection with changes of order in the cosmology of the journey.'

This, to my mind, is scholarly soup. It means nothing. Why do I venerate Dante? Certainly not because of his visions mystical, sightseeing or his Christianity, but because he is the most accomplished poet technically that has probably ever written. *The Divine Comedy* succeeds not because Dante was a mystic, but because he drew largely, as Byron did in *Childe Harold*, on his own experience and consequent suffering. His imagery is always a bull's eye. As a technician we have nobody in England to match him except perhaps for the immaculate Pope. Dante should be read, and first published.

Appendix v

The Ars Poetae
being a crib for Bucket

What is Poetry?

It is a communication. (Think of your Communion in
the Catholic Service to perceive what the word communication means.) The thing communicated need not
necessarily be from the poet to the people; it can be
a communication from the poets' perception to his
understanding. But whether it is a communication from
one part of himself to another, or from him to other
people: it can only be judged by assessing the validity or
truth of what the poem says and the effectiveness with
which it says it.

Poetry is Not:

mere decoration to thought or embroidery upon the
structure of drama.

not an effusion like tea, but the Essence, i.e. the irredu-
cible minimum.

not necessarily a pretty picture of an herbaceous border;
a bloody sunset or a mere collection of images, rimes or
regular or monotonous lines.

it does not exist in counting syllables.
it does not exist in rimes or muddled metaphor
    nor in ambiguities
      not certainly as a trifle for 'leisure'.

Poetry is:

The point at which Consciousness grows
    At which sensitivity seeks
It is a discovery of sensibility
    Where thoughts and feeling
    supported by experience and
    observation extend our
    range of living, perception.
A good poem
    Adds
  to human experience
It tells us something
    we didnt know before
    didnt feel before
    hadnt seen ourselves before
    but After
    will know, feel and see for ourselves.
A good poem
    Adds to us.

On the other 'and
    A bad poem
pretends to be what it aint
Clothing itself in
    second-hand verbal clothing

poetical clutter
rimes
flowers
ambiguities
and muddle
it thinks nothing
feels not for itself
and adds nowt to us

And, dear daughter, dont think
poetry is:
just verbal patterns;
three bricks placed correctly
can be a poem;
a loaf of bread (black)
is a poem;
good coffee is a poem.
Poetry is a creation.
All men are poets if they only knew it – not necessarily
in words (D.G.)

And may you be damned
if you use poetry
        as something to hand on your wall;
        preserve for birth, marriages or death;
        to impress your neighbours or
        yourself;
        as part of bloody 'culture'
        i.e. a thing apart from
        living.
                mere doodling for
        leisure.

Lastly use your instinct
i.e. the poem you can
make use of – which Adds
to you, which tells you
something and becomes an
adjunct, an extension of
yourself is valuable.

That poem which
dont, discard

its better to sweep the stairs
or plant daffodils
than read nine tenths of literature.

But before you decide
you can live in the
future without the poet
and poetry, consider what
you would think
  how much you would
  feel
  to whom
  and how youd pray
if he hadnt first
  felt
  shown
  knelt
  known
and showed you the way.

Humanity, Madame, is of
no consequence
except for its consciousness
and that consciousness
    that awareness
    that waking
has been in the poem
    by the poem
    and is the poem.

The Ronald Duncan Papers: the New Collection

Appendix vi

English Appreciation

A

The aim of this book is to give the student of English Literature the critical tools to appreciate an access whether on poems or passages of prose are good or bad.

The author is himself a poet and playwright who has devoted forty years to composition. He also took the English Tripos at Cambridge University.

In the first part of the book, he prints various poems and passages taken from novels without naming their well-known authors; in the second part, he assesses these examples with which they may be faced.

B

Before you can evaluate literature you have to know what it is. The same goes for music. Is literature to be confined to pretty and innocuous verses about nature, amorous hopes or rejection, incoherent subjective hosannahs? Critics as eminent as T. S. Eliot, F. R. Leavis and Pound have been content to accept those absurd confines and restrictions. It is our purpose to open the windows for Literature to let in the whole of consciousness and communication. To accept its present limitations is as

absurd as restricting music to the mere vibration of cat-
gut or to confine chemistry to the analysis of calcium
compounds.

C

One of the reasons why poetry is so little read today is
that it has become irrelevant. It tells us little: that a rose
is a rose is a rose as Gertrude Stein put it; it decorates
perhaps but fails to enlarge the potentials of our being.
Bad poetry can be merely pretty, great poetry must be
painful and disturbing. Man grows from pain not
pleasure. Good poetry should disturb. A great poem
is something which makes us different than the person
we were before reading it.

This is not to argue that Literature should be political
or concerned with any particular political fallacy. On the
contrary. Politics is the mistaken purpose since Hegel
and Marx of subjecting the individual to the needs of the
state. We believe that human consciousness only glows
through the individual and the function of Literature is
to nurture that growth. It is a communication not
necessarily from the poet or novelist to a large audience.
But a communication from one part of his mind to
another – to which we are privileged to eavesdrop. . . .

The Ronald Duncan Papers: the New Collection

Appendix vii

Words

In the beginning was the word. A word is a swipe at the
inarticulate undergrowth. There can be no consciousness
without the word. It is not that words are merely the
tools of thought; they are thought itself; without them
vacancy.

Each word is a metaphor for a thing, and the essence
of a thing is its ability to act. The most active words are
verbs, and the best nouns suggest an action. Consciousness is extended by the formation creation [*sic*] of new
words. When a language stops adding to its vocabulary it
is a dead language. Dictionaries are like tombs; the dead
deserve respect but new words have to be born, coined if
a language is to remain current.

For an exercise imagine existence without language.
Imagine consciousness struggling inarticulate without the
word to swing on. What were the first words that were
formed? Perhaps the terror as trees lit into flame made
primitive man's cry coin the word fire. Perhaps his
wandering thirsty over the waste kneed him to cry water.
Then later, as his dumb tongue became a nimble instru-
ment for thought, new words came to his lips as his
hands created the things for his needs.

Take the word 'scythe' for instance, you can hear in
its syllables the sounds of the blade cutting through the

weeds. The word 'plate' is flat. The word 'wheel' revolves. Write out a dozen words which are onomatopoeic, that is, their sounds suggest their use. Saxon words are particularly near to the reality they describe, that is to say their metaphor is contained in their sound.

Human consciousness nudges forward on the elbows of its words. There can be no development, extension of human potential, unless we coin a word to pin that extension. Shades of feeling, sharpening of sensibilities need new words to define the new territory. The Greeks had no word for compassion, Christianity added this word, and in doing so extended human sensitivity. If we cannot describe our feelings the danger is we may cease to have those feelings. That is why poetry is important, and the really creative act for a poet is the poem which is a new word.

Languages can be poor in the most awkward places; for instance the French have a word for deep, but no word for shallow: they have to say not deep. The Greeks had two words for love, *eros* and *agippe*, English is poor in this respect. We talk about loving a woman, loving ice-cream, loving to play football. When we have to use one word to cover such a range of feelings we fail to express our true meaning. The result is emotional chaos, clumsiness, the tool not being fit for the job in hand. A word can be as blunt as a chisel, as inadequate as a hammer if you have to drive a screw in.

Again, it is noticeable that in war, when people's urgency is aroused, when they are driven by circumstances to express themselves, new words are formed. We call it slang, and speak of it derogatorily. We should not. All words were slang when they were sharp with meaning. Perhaps young people intuitively realise the poverty of our language when, instead of talking about liking somebody, they say they have a yen for somebody. Perhaps this is an attempt to define their precise feelings.

In the beginning was the word. Try to think of three or four states of being which cannot be described by a single word, and then coin a word to describe that experience, so that one word will do where three or four have previously been necessary. For example, we have all experienced the state of being when we are not asleep and we are not awake. Try to coin a word to fit this common experience without using a negative. Find two other common experiences and coin verbs to suit them.

A noun that is most active suggests a verb. For instance, the word tiger implies ferocity lying in wait for stalking, and the final spring. You could write 'He lay in wait for his prey like a tiger', but if you wrote simply, 'He tigered his prey', and used the noun as a verb, greater immediacy is obtained. Coin half a dozen verbs in this way, and write sentences round them.

Cut out clumsy metaphor convention: 'such and such is like so and so' or 'as so and so'. By driving the connection 'so and so' into an adjective attached to 'such and such' or, better still, making 'such and such' absorb its affinity with 'so and so' and make a new noun out of the perceived relationship.

For example, the lines:

Autumn like a pheasant's tail
lifts over the hedge

contains the conventional formula for metaphor; but a
more immediate method to show the connection between
'autumn' and 'a pheasant's tail' would be to write:

> *The pheasant's tail of autumn*
> *lifts over the hedge*

but better still the visual connection can be given greater
immediacy if you write:

> *Pheasant's tail autumn*
> *lifts over the hedge.*

Yet in both of these we have achieved nothing more than
an adjective whereas language is more creative when it
makes a new noun (thing) and most creative when it
makes a new verb (an act). The dynamic of words is the
dynamic of the spirit. And the energy, activity, of the
parts of speech can be given in the following order
showing diminishing potential:

> verb
>
> noun
>
> adverb
>
> adjective
>
> preposition.

If the verb is right, the rest of the sentence is driven to
meaning. If you can't find the right verb, make it; carve it
out of the lumpy dumbness; use your tongue as a chisel.
Every word is a metaphor for a thing or a condition of a
thing. But a verb gives the thing being ('to be' derives
from the Aryan — 'to grow'). With this in mind, we can
look at the sentence:

Autumn like a pheasant's tail
lifts over the hedge

again and attempt to be more creative. If we write:

Pheasant-autumn
lifts over the hedge

we achieve a noun in which the metaphor is implied. But
we have lost the explicit connection between the colours
of autumn and the colours of the pheasant's tail. But
this connection is no great loss in meaning. For it is
impossible to think of autumn or pheasant without
visualising their colours.

But now, if we remember, the creative importance of
the verb and look at the sentence again, we could write:

Pheasant-autumn
tails over the hedge.

The new verb gives the visual image. But the sentence
is still not perfect, i.e. carrying maximum charge of
meaning within minimum number of words. (Good
poetry is like a good telegram.) The new compound noun
is clumsy.

So, let us look at the sentence for the last time. Let us
concentrate our metaphor wholly within the act, within
the verb, and write:

Autumn pheasants over the hedge.

But even now we can achieve greater concision because
the preposition is implicit within the verb. We all know

not only a pheasant's colouring but how the bird moves too. Therefore it is possible to drive the sentence to:

Autumn pheasants the hedge.

And give the metaphor wholly *in charge* of the verb. This achieves an ideogram (cf. Fenollosa).

Do not worry about grammar. The grammarians are concerned with rules. Rules define conditions which are not changing. Language must change, if it is alive. If our language is dead, so are we. Do not worry about grammar: make it.

The Ronald Duncan Papers: the New Collection

Appendix viii

Unpublished Typescript

It is preferable to hang yourself than be beheaded with a
bread knife. I had hoped that it would not be necessary to
write another volume of autobiography. I do so in self-
defence, believing it is preferable to attack oneself than
be silent and thus encourage others to invent libels, or
untruths, which they peddle behind my back. There is
one such piece of biography on my desk at the moment.
In it the author describes me as 'a devout Catholic who
went around with a missal in his pocket. . . . ' I have never
been a catholic; I have never carried a missal. Indeed,
I count myself a practising atheist since the age of
sixteen. I could give a few dozen instances of similar
nonsensical journalistic truths. Far better to be an enemy
to myself, than depend on calumny of my friends who
have not met me. Such as the young lady, now going
about London, telling people she is my mistress when
I have not even met her, let alone suffered the rigours of
her predatory embrace. Surely I have paid tribute enough
in that area? But it seems women will go to any length to
share your bad reputation, even though the only comfort
lies in the orbit of their empty heads.

So amongst other things let me admit my relationship
with ———— before well-subsidised and assiduous PhDs
do her reputation more harm than I did myself.

I first saw her in 1953 at a party in Bude. She was about twenty. I did not know her name, nor from where she came. Nobody introduced us. This to my annoyance because I was most attracted by her, her dark hair and scarlet dress.

The party was given by the late Doctor Holding and his wife. The purpose: to allow me an opportunity to appeal for funds for the Taw and Torridge Festival of the Arts which I was then trying to found.

There were so many people in the house, both upstairs and downstairs, that my hostess told me I had two alternatives: either to give a speech on each floor, or to spout one from the staircase so that both floors could hear me simultaneously. I chose the latter course and delivered my oration to an empty staircase [feeling] more than unusually foolish, not unaware that the financial donations would be as void as the people in front of me.

After this effort, I went downstairs in search of the red dress only to find the girl had gone. I asked my daughter, Briony, who the girl was. She did not believe I did not know. 'That was ——— ,' she said, 'I've known her for years, she lives not more than three miles from us.'

'It's odd I've never met her', I complained.

'That's easily dealt with,' my daughter said, 'I'll ask her to our Christmas party we're giving next week!'

I looked forward to this occasion with rare tolerance of Briony's prodigious social appetite. But much to my disappointment, ——— never came. I never reasoned why. Probably I've had a previous disappointment. . . .

We returned to London soon after this and ———'s image receded from my overburden[ed] mind.

The Ronald Duncan Papers: the New Collection

Appendix ix

Letter to Richard Findlater

22nd March, 1982

Dear Mr Findlater,

Your book entitled *At the Royal Court, 25 Years of the English Stage Company* came into my hands for the first time only last week.

I telephoned *The Observer* to speak to you and left a message to call me back. I also did this to the Director of the Royal Court with a similar lack of response.

I would have thought that since I founded the English Stage Company out of my own pocket and became its first Chairman it would have been expedient of you to have consulted me while you were writing your book to avoid the most glaring errors, or at least to have had the courtesy to have sent me a copy when it was published.

I have not got the entire book even now but various pages in which you refer to me. On page 14 you write: 'In contrast with Duncan's rightish, high church ideals'. How accurate is this? I was the Communist delegate for the Arts Society for Cambridge University to the Brussels conference and later I wrote, with Alan Bush, the March for the Rhondda miners to sing when they converged on London. And did I not invite Oscar Lewenstein, a Communist, to join the Council?

As for me being High Church, I have been a practising atheist since the age of ten. It is true that I wrote *This Way to the Tomb* for the Pilgrim Players and *Our Lady's Tumbler* was commissioned by Salisbury Cathedral for the Festival of Britain. In these circumstances did you expect me to write on a Buddhist theme?

On the same page you say that I founded the theatre in order to produce my own plays. The original leaflet with its emblem designed by John Piper and now on my desk lists the following playwrights: T. S. Eliot, Christopher Fry, Peter Ustinov, Evelyn Waugh, Graham Greene, John Whiting. These were not all poetic dramas, though it is true that T. S. Eliot offered to write a play and George Devine refused to discuss it with him.

On page 16 you say that Neville Blond advanced £8,000, you will find this in error. On page 28 it is categorically stated that I put in so much hard work to create the English Stage Company as a platform for my own work. Surely the agreement of Topolski, Epstein, Minten and others to design sets and Benjamin Britten offering to write a pantomime for the Stage Company rather undermines this contention of yours. On another page, number not given, you state that: 'Duncan believed him to have deliberately sabotaged his work. From then on Duncan regarded him (Devine) as an enemy.'

If you had bothered to contact me I could have told you why I became suspicious of Devine. 1. He referred in my presence to Neville Blond as being 'a Jew seeking a knighthood who ought to be milked,' 2. He referred to my friend Lord Harewood as being an 'empty-headed Earl'.

These remarks did not endear me to him, especially when I found he fudged his accounts in at least one instance as Lord Harewood would confirm. In view of the above defamation I must ask you to insert an errata slip in the present edition or withdraw it to make certain that all these errors are rectified in any subsequent edition, and unless I have your assurance to this effect I shall instruct my solicitor to issue a writ against you and your publishing company for defamation or damages.

The Ronald Duncan Papers: the New Collection

Appendix x

Artistic Policy
of the English Stage Company

I have delayed writing this for two years. I do so now
as Founder of the English Stage Company. Since it was
I who recommended our present Artistic Director for the
post I feel I have a responsibility towards the Council,
and should explain why I am profoundly dissatisfied with
our Artistic Policy.

What were our original aims? They were:

1.   To present new plays without bias towards any
     political or religious doctrine, neither excluding the
     realistic play nor the more imaginative drama.
2.   To achieve some stylisation in both acting and
     décor.
3.   To react against the box-set, and the naturalistic
     décor which made productions so expensive that
     Managements could not afford to risk the produc-
     tion of experimental plays.

When I originally approached George Devine before his
appointment he expressed his complete agreement with
all of my views, and the aims stated above. But after
his appointment it became apparent that he in fact did
not agree.

It is true that we have received public acclaim and are regarded as a successful enterprise. Perhaps this is the time when we should indulge in self-criticism?

The success we have is due in a large degree to two factors.

1. The company has been efficiently and effectively promoted and nursed by our Chairman.
2. There was a great need for an experimental theatre after all the small theatres in London closed down. Consequently the Press has bent over backwards to help us. Praise has come from all sides. At a time of famine people do not look twice at stale bread.

In spite of the public acclaim we have received artists themselves are not impressed with our achievement. Why?

1. Our Artistic Direction, wearing the shawl of the late Mrs Webb, and the spectacles of the late G. D. H. Cole, has made no creative contribution to the theatre. It has merely presented the kind of plays in Sloane Square during the 1950s which were presented in the small London theatres during the 1930s.

    The only new note is to be found in the vein of satire shown in Nigel Dennis's *Cards of Identity* and that in Simpson's *One Way Pendulum*. We have allowed ourselves to be bemused by Osborne's commercial success. Though he has a general talent, it is a mistake to equate commercial success with artistic achievement. Though exceptions can be found we have constantly produced plays of a social realistic kind as though we had just heard of Ibsen. Clifford Odets wrote *Waiting for Lefty* over a generation ago. Creative artists are unimpressed by an organisation which fails to do much more than make reprints. A theatre which produces an opportunity for a clique is a different thing from a theatre which is actively creative. We have made a revolution in *fashion* which is a different thing from a revolution in *taste*.

My complaints against the New Establishment in Sloane Square are:

1. Plays are only considered from a polemical point of view. Their political bias is as obvious as it is outdated. The tilts against the Establishment are reminiscent of undergraduate larks. We achieve facetiousness and a lame frivolity; our wit lacks edge, our satire is insufficient to cause discomfort. It pretends to be revolutionary. But it is a revolution which took place when Auden was 23.

2. With our eyes on the political content of the plays we entirely ignore the language in which they are written.

3. Plays by competent playwrights which do not conform to the provincialism of Sloane Square are dismissed before they can be considered by the Artistic Committee, i.e. the plays of people like N. C. Hunter, Bernard Kops, Dennis Canan, John Whiting, Christopher Fry, Peter Ustinov etc.

I believe Mr. Devine stated that 'for us to present Christopher Fry's new play would have been to surrender to the Establishment'. What artistic principles lie behind such silly prejudice? Whatever the faults of this particular play are, our Artistic Director's comment shows a limited perspective.

4. When the Council last debated artistic policy the following Minute was recorded, dated 5th May 1958:

    1. That the preliminary readers of manuscripts should be changed at frequent intervals to avoid any similarity of minds reading plays submitted.

    2. That established playwrights and writers should be approached with greater energy to write for the Royal Court Theatre.

    3. That every effort should be made to encourage writers of different points of view so as to widen the general artistic scope of the productions presented.

    4. That the Artistic Directors should get out to the provincial repertory companies to see new plays and performers.

To what degree has that resolution been implemented? The Artistic Committee is still generally in the quandary of having to choose between two plays, neither of which they are particularly enthusiastic about, because the Artistic Director is only offering them plays which he wishes to do. Having attended most meetings of this committee it is my conclusion that it is a rubber stamp.

What should the English Stage Company be doing?

The theatre of Ibsen and Shaw was important when there was no Welfare State. If there were no other issues other than materialism or social questions, then these two dramatists have said all there is to be said.

But that is not the case. The theatre is even more important today now that we have discovered that materialism has brought us to the precipice of the H-Bomb, and left humanity blindly seeking other values.

The theatre has to be the operating theatre in which the diseases of the age can be examined and amputated. The modern playwright has to be a surgeon; a priest without a religion; a psychiatrist without a couch. And he has to perform his operations under the anaesthetic of entertainment.

The playwright has to express not what is already known but articulate the dilemmas of human consciousness before they are realised by the mass of people.

The real subject matter, the keel of the plays of the 1960s, should not be the outmoded class struggles of the 1930s but related to the spiritual crisis that we all stand in today.

What is this crisis?

One could say that man now finds himself *alone*. For the first time in the whole history of human consciousness man is aware that he has to be self-reliant, that he is entirely dependant on his own humanity. All other eras have had their gods, modern man has killed those gods. He has to face up to the torment of being the only conscious thing in an unconscious universe. Having destroyed the god outside himself, he has now to create a god inside himself.

The Renaissance or the Elizabethan age flowered because of a geographical expansion. Our own era has achieved a geophysical expansion, but a spiritual and psychic contraction. Though our horizon has been expanded by sputniks, our orbit has contracted to the distance between our two ears.

King Lear was driven mad on a heath. Modern man is going mad in a centrally-heated luxury flat.

The Church, the orthodoxies, have completely failed to re-orient themselves. No guidance will come from ostriches like Dr Fisher.

The plays of the sixties will not be modern plays unless they face *some* of these issues.

For the E.S.C. to have a morbid fixation on class warfare and sociology in this era is as relevant as if we were looking for plays about drawbridges and moats. If sociology is enough and we wish to be contemporary in those terms, we should commission a play now on the theme of the traffic problem. At least that would be constructive.

We are trailing along behind Shaw and Brecht as though Jung, Watts or Heidegger had never existed, or we had never heard of Frobenius.

The Lily White Boys our present production is an imitation of *The Threepenny Opera* which was written in the 1920s. A reprint.

If materialism is all-important then the best that can be said for our policy is that it is covered in cobwebs. But if materialism is not all important then we have to find other values. We do not even dare look for them. Why?

I am NOT suggesting that we should present what is known as Religious Drama.

I am NOT suggesting that we should present Poetic Drama.

It IS a question of presenting serious modern plays, and no serious modern play could be without an implicit religious or poetic content.

The idea that religion is something to do with *Hymns Ancient and Modern* is as naive and stupid as the putrid notion that poetry is something to do with lyricism about daffodils. Religion is where we are, poetry is our ticket.

I am NOT making a plea for tragedies, there is nothing so serious as comedy.

There is no doubt that our present Artistic Director has a very considerable *administrative* talent. But the ideal Director for the E.S.C. should have a more creative bent. It is too much to hope that we can find the equivalent of a Diaghilev, a person who, without any creative [*sic*] of his own, was able to perceive it in others, and put a Cocteau in touch with a Stravinsky. But it is not too much [to] hope that we could find somebody who is aware of contemporary trends in art.

It is my opinion that any artistic director would be milked out of creative ideas after two years.

The suggestion that our present Director should be given leave of absence of six months or a year, while his Assistant holds the fort until he returns for another year is one which I deprecate most strongly.

The Ronald Duncan Papers: the New Collection

Notes

A Highly Personal Foreword

1. Lockyear, Harold, ed., *A Tribute to Ronald Duncan by His Friends*, Harton Press, 1974, p. 34.

2. Ibid., p.83.

3. Duncan, Ronald, *Obsessed*, Michael Joseph, 1977.

4. Duncan, Ronald, *All Men Are Islands*, Rupert Hart-Davis, 1964.

5. Duncan, Ronald, *How to Make Enemies*, Rupert Hart-Davis, 1968.

6. Hogg, James, ed., *Ronald Duncan: Verse Dramatist and Poet Interviewed*, University of Salzburg, 1973, p. 31.

7. Moat, J., *Welcome Overtures, Stages of Solar Eclipse, The Ballad of the Leat*, Dartington Poetry Press, 1987, p. 57, VII (three stanzas), in which Rose-Marie is mentioned, and p. 56, Rose-Marie, the poet's wife.

8. Lockyear, Harold, ed., op. cit., p. 77.

1 Criticism and Biography

1. See Appendix i, p. 77.

2. Eliot, T. S., 'The Frontiers of Criticism', in *On Poetry and Poets*, Faber, 1957, pp. 111-12.

3. Duncan, Ronald, *All Men Are Islands*, Rupert Hart-Davis, 1964, p. 158.

4. See 'English with Tears', Appendix iii, p. 81.

5. Eliot, T. S., ed., 'A Few Don'ts', in *Literary Essays of Ezra Pound*, Faber, 1954, p. 4.

6. Eliot, T. S., 'The Frontiers of Criticism', in *On Poetry and Poets*, Faber, 1957, p. 103.

7. Duncan, Ronald, *Selected Lyrics and Satires of the Earl of Rochester*, Rebel Press, 1980, pp. 14-23.

8. Eliot, T. S., 'The Function of Criticism', in *On Poetry and Poets*, Faber, 1957, p. 103, footnote 2.

9. Duncan, Ronald, *The Solitudes and Other Poems*, Faber, 1960.

10. Lockyear, H., ed., *A Tribute to Ronald Duncan by His Friends*, Harton Press, 1974, p. 76.

11. Newton, K. M., 'The Formalist Critic', in *Twentieth Century Literary Theory: a Reader*, Macmillan, 1988, p. 46.

2 Poetry and Ronald Duncan's Views on Form

1. Newton, K. M., 'Formalist Criticism: Its Principles and Limits', in *Twentieth Century Literary Theory*, Macmillan, 1988, p. 50.

2. Duncan, Ronald, *For the Few*, Rebel Press, 1977, p. 56.

3. Newton, K. M., 'Object Feeling and Judgement', in *Twentieth Century Literary Theory*, Macmillan, 1988, pp. 71-2.

4. The proper title is Dame Helen Gardner.

5. Bergonzi, Bernard, *The Myth of Modernism and Twentieth Century Literature*, St Martin's Press, New York, 1986, p. 113.

6. See Appendix iii, p. 86.

7. Dante, *De Vulgari Eloquentia*, Rebel Press, 1980, p. 10.

8. See 'English with Tears', Appendix iii, p. 82.

9. See 'The Ars Poetae', Appendix v, p. 90. A slightly different versions appears as 'The Technique of Poetry'.

10. See 'English Appreciation', Appendix vi, p. 95.

11. Ibid.

12. Duncan, Ronald, *Unpopular Poems*, Rupert Hart-Davis, 1969, p. 21.

13. Ibid., p. 24.

14. See 'Words', Appendix vii, p. 97.

15. Wahl, W. B., *Ronald Duncan: Dramatist and Poet Interviewed*, Institut für Englischesprache und Literatur, Saltzburg, 1973, p. 51.

16. Ibid., p. 164.

17. Eliot, T. S., ed., *Literary Essays of Ezra Pound*, Faber, 1954.

18. Wahl, W. B., op. cit., p. 17.

19. Duncan, Ronald, *Obsessed*, Michael Joseph, 1957, p. 115.

20. Duncan, Ronald, *All Men Are Islands*, Rupert Hart-Davis, 1964, p. 100.

21. Ibid., p. 102.

22. Ibid., p. 204.

23. Wahl, W. B., op. cit., p. 50.

24. Duncan, Ronald, *Selected Poems, 1940-71*, Rebel Press, 1978.

25. Duncan, Ronald, *The Solitudes and Other Poems*, Faber, 1960.

26. Duncan, Ronald, *Obsessed*, Michael Joseph, 1957, p. 247.

27. Ibid., p. 248.

28. Reid, John, in Lockyear, H., ed., *Tribute to Ronald Duncan by His Friends*, Harton Press, 1974, p. 12 – only one of several references to this label.

29. Duncan, Ronald, *Judas*, Anthony Blond, 1960.

30. Duncan, Ronald, *Man*, Rebel Press, 1970, Part I, pp. 9-10.

31. Wilson, Colin, in Lockyear, H., ed., *A Tribute to Ronald Duncan by His Friends*, Harton Press, 1974, p. 95.

32. Duncan, Ronald, *The Mongrel and Other Poems*, Faber. 1960.

33. Wahl, W. B., op. cit., p. 91.

34. Murphy, Richard, 'Two Poets', *The Spectator*, 21 July 1950.

35. Blacksell, J., in Lockyear, H., ed., op. cit., p. 102.

36. *Times Literary Supplement*, 4 August 1950.

37. Wilson, Colin, op. cit., p. 85.

3 The Significance of Duncan's Autobiographies

1. Duncan, Ronald, *How to Make Enemies*, Rupert Hart-Davis, 1968.

2. Duncan, Ronald, *The Complete Pacifist*, Boriswood, 1937.

3. Kingsley, Charles, *Westward Ho!*, Robinson Publishers, 1989, p. 113.

4. The source is Rose-Marie Duncan, as confirmed in Duncan, Ronald, *How To Make Enemies* Rupert Hart-Davis, 1964, p. 338.

5. Duncan, Ronald, unpublished (8 September 1969).

6. Duncan, Ronald, Log Book, unpublished (1982).

7. Ibid.

8. See Appendix viii, p. 103.

9. Duncan, Ronald, *Obsessed*, Michael Joseph, 1977, p. 115.

10. Duncan, Ronald, unpublished manuscript.

11. More 'enemies' are made later in the field of drama and the English Stage Company, to which reference will be made in Chapter Five.

12. Lockyear, H., ed., *A Tribute to Ronald Duncan by His Friends*, p. 77 (as used in 'A Highly Personal Foreword').

13. Ibid., p. 78.

14. Duncan, Ronald, unpublished diary, 8 February 1968.

15. Ibid.

16. Duncan, Ronald, *Obsessed*, Michael Joseph, 1977, p. 37.

17. Ibid., p. 27.

18. Ibid., p. 28.

19. Ibid., p. 52.

20. Ibid., p. 92.

21. Ibid., p. 22.

22. Duncan, Ronald, *Judas*, Anthony Blond, 1960, p. 28.

23. Duncan, Ronald, 'Introduction', *Selected Lyrics and Satires of the Earl of Rochester*, Rebel Press, p. 10.

24. See Appendix i, p. 77.

25. Duncan, Ronald, unpublished diary.

26. Unpublished sketches.

27. Perhaps from ancient folklore, where the mother pelican was thought to pierce her breast with her bill and thus feed her young with her own blood, as in 'Those Pelican Daughters', Hunter, E. K., ed., *King Lear*, Act III, Penguin, 1972, p. 72. The pelican is thus a creature of self-sacrifice.

28. Eliot, T. S., 'The Frontiers of Criticism', in *On Poetry and Poets*, Faber, 1957, pp. 111-112.

4   A Prolific Writer of Great Diversity

1. Duncan, Ronald, *Jan's Journals*, William Campion, 1949.

2. Duncan, Ronald, *Jan at the Blue Fox*, Museum Press, 1952.

3. Herbert Gunn, Editor of the *Evening Standard*.

4. Duncan, Ronald, *Jan's Journal*, William Campion, 1949, p. 20.

5. Duncan, Ronald, *Journal of a Husbandman*, Faber, 1944.

6. Duncan, Ronald, *How to Make Enemies*, Rupert Hart-Davis, 1968, p. 170.

7. Ibid., p. 170.

8. Ibid., p. 28.

9. Haueter, M. W., *Ronald Duncan: the Metaphysical Content of his Plays*, Rebel Press, 1969.

10. Duncan, Ronald, 'What the Critics Said about *Jan at the Blue Fox*', in *Jan at the Blue Fox*, Museum Press, 1952.

11. Ibid., p. 101.

12. Duncan, Ronald, *Home Made Home*, Faber, 1957, p. 13.

13. Ibid., p. 19.

14. Ibid., p. 14.

15. Ibid., p. 152.

16. *Townsman*, No. 21, July 1944, Kraus Reprint, 1972.

17. Duncan, Ronald, *Gandhi: Selected Writings*, Harper and Row, 1971.

18. Duncan, Ronald, *Working with Britten: a Personal Memoir*, Rebel Press, 1981.

19. Ibid., p. 9.

20. Duncan, Ronald, and Weston-Smith, M., *The Encyclopaedia of Ignorance*, Pergamon Press, 1977.

21. Duncan, Ronald, and Weston-Smith, M., *The Encylopaedia of Medical Ignorance*, Pergamon Press, 1984.

22. Duncan, Ronald, and Harris, Melvin, 'Introduction', *Lying Truths*, Penguin Press, 1979.

23. Duncan, Ronald, *How to Make Enemies*, Rupert Hart-Davis, 1965, p. 373.

24. Duncan, Ronald, *Critics' Gaffes*, Macdonald, 1983, p. 24.

25. Bahr, Herman, in Duncan, Ronald, *Critics' Gaffes*, op. cit.

26. Pepper, John Henry, in Duncan, Ronald, *Critics' Gaffes*, op. cit.

27. Duncan, Ronald, and Wilson, Colin, *Marx Refuted: the Verdict of History*, Ashgrove Press, 1987.

28. Williams, M., ed., *My Cornwall*, Bossiney Books, 1973.

29. Duncan, Ronald, *All Men Are Islands*, Rupert Hart-Davis, 1964, p. 179.

30. Turner, James, ed., *Unlikely Ghosts*, Taplinger, 1969.

31. Turner, James, ed., *Fourth Ghost Book*, Pan Books, 1965.

32. Baker, Denys Val, ed., *Cornish Short Stories*, Penguin, 1976.

33. Duncan, Ronald, *The Perfect Mistress*, Rupert Hart-Davis, 1969.

34. Ibid., cover.

35. Duncan, Ronald, *The Last Adam*, Dennis Dobson, 1961, p. 40.

36. Duncan, Ronald, *Mr and Mrs Mouse*, Rebel Press, 1977, p. 6.

37. Duncan, Ronald, *Tale of Tails and Other Stories*, Rebel Press, 1981.

38. Duncan, Ronald, *Mr and Mrs Mouse*, op. cit..

39. Duncan, Ronald, *The Last Adam*, Dennis Dobson, 1961, p. 81.

40. Duncan, Ronald, *How to Make Enemies*, Rupert Hart-Davis, 1968, p. 46.

41. Ibid.

42. Although no direct connection can be made here with the pelican theme, an indirect imagery is possibly present in this line.

5 Drama and Criticism

1. Duncan, Ronald, *How to Make Enemies*, Rupert Hart-Davis, 1968, p. 172.

2. Beverley Baxter, *Evening Standard*.

3. Duncan, Ronald, op. cit., p. 334.

4. Ibid.

5. Ibid.

6. *Stage*, 18 October 1945. See Duncan's transcripts of reviews from a press cuttings album, Appendix ii, p. 79.

7. *Weekly Review*, 18 October 1965.

8. *The Observer*, 14 October 1945.

9. Duncan, Ronald, op. cit., p. 154.

10. Letter from Edmund Blunden to Ronald Duncan, 4 December 1945, unpublished.

11. *Evening Standard*, 3 November 1945.

12. Duncan, Ronald, op. cit., p. 156.

13. Lockyear, H., ed., *A Tribute to Ronald Duncan by His Friends*, Harton Press, 1974, pp. 8-13.

14. Ibid., p. 20.

15. Hinchliffe, Arnold P., *Modern Verse Drama*, Methuen, 1977, pp. 31-35.

16. Ibid., p. 36.

17. Wahl, W. B., *Ronald Duncan: Verse Dramatist Interviewed*, Institut für Englischesprache und Literatur, Saltzburg, p. 132.

18. Haueter, Max Walter, *Ronald Duncan: the Metaphysical Content of His Plays*, Rebel Press, 1969, p. 48.

19. Duncan, Ronald, *Obsessed*, Rupert Hart-Davis, 1968, p. 43.

20. Duncan, Ronald, *How to Make Enemies*, Rupert Hart-Davis, 1968, p. 173.

21. Duncan, Ronald, *Collected Plays*, Rupert Hart-Davis, 1971, p. 150.

22. Letter from Deborah Kerr to Ronald Duncan, unpublished.

23. Wilson, C., in Lockyear, H., ed., *A Tribute to Ronald Duncan by His Friends*, Harton Press, 1974, p. 90.

24. Haueter, Max Walter, op. cit., p. 133.

25. Findlater, Richard, *Twenty-Five Years of the English Stage Company at the Royal Court*, Amber Lane Press, 1981, cover.

26. Letter from Ronald Duncan to Richard Findlater, 22 March 1982, Appendix ix, p. 105.

27. 'Notes on Artistic Policy of the English Stage Company', Appendix x, p. 108.

28. Duncan, Ronald, unpublished.

29. Duncan, Ronald, *All Men Are Islands*, Rupert Hart-Davis, 1964, p. 73.

Bibliography

Primary Sources

Scrap Book of Press Cuttings.
Diaries and Log Books, No 4.
Letters.

> All included by kind permission of the Ronald Duncan
> Literary Foundation.

Duncan, Ronald, *The Complete Pacifist* (Boriswood, 1937).
    Journal of a Husbandman (Faber, 1944).
    'The Scythe', *Townsman*, Nos. 21-24 (1944-45).
    Home Made Home (Faber, 1947).
    Jan's Journal (William Campion, 1949).
    The Mongrel and Other Poems (Faber, 1950).
    The Last Adam (Dennis Dobson, 1952).
    Jan at the Blue Fox (Museum Press, 1952).
    Judas (Anthony Blond, 1960).
    The Solitudes and Other Poems (Faber, 1960).
    Saint Spiv (Dennis Dobson, 1961).
    All Men Are Islands, (Rupert Hart-Davis, 1964).
    How to Make Enemies (Rupert Hart-Davis, 1968).
    Unpopular Poems (Rupert Hart-Davis, 1969).
    The Perfect Mistress (Rupert Hart-Davis, 1969).
    Man, Parts 1 to 5 (Rebel Press, 1970–1974).
    Collected Plays (Rupert Hart-Davis, 1971).

Gandhi: Selected Writings (Harper and Row, 1971).

Obsessed (Michael Joseph, 1977).

For the Few (Rebel Press, 1977).

Mr and Mrs Mouse, with drawings by Rose-Marie Duncan (Rebel Press, 1977).

Selected Poems, 1940-1971 (Rebel Press, 1978).

Dante: De Vulgari Eloquentia (Rebel Press, 1980).

Selected Lyrics and Satires of the Earl of Rochester (Rebel Press, 1980).

Working with Britten: a Personal Memoir (Rebel Press, 1981).

The Tail of Tales and Other Stories (Rebel Press, 1981).

Duncan, R., and Wilson, C., *Marx Refuted: the Verdict of History* (Bath: Ashgrove Press, 1987).

Duncan, R., and Weston-Smith, M., *The Encyclopedia of Ignorance: Life Sciences and Earth Sciences* (Pergamon Press, 1977).

Lying Truths (Pergamon Press, 1979).

The Encylopaedia of Medical Ignorance (Pergamon Press, 1984).

Duncan, R., Harris, M., and Joliffe, G., *Critics' Gaffes* (Macdonald, 1983).

Secondary Sources

Baker, Denys Val., ed., *Cornish Short Stories* (Penguin, 1976).

Bergonzi, B., *The Myth of Modernism and Twentieth Century Literature* (New York: St Martin's Press, 1986).

Eliot, T. S., ed., *Literary Essays of Ezra Pound* (Faber, 1954).

Eliot, T. S., *On Poetry and Poets* (Faber, 1957).

Findlater, R., ed., *At the Royal Court: Twenty-Five Years of the English Stage Company* (Amber Lane Press, 1981).

Haueter, M. W., *Ronald Duncan: the Metaphysical Content of His Plays* (Rebel Press, 1969).

Hinchliffe, Arnold P., *Modern Verse Drama* (Methuen, 1977).

Hunter, G. K., ed., *Shakespeare: King Lear* (Penguin, 1972).

Kingsley, C., *Westward Ho!* (Robinson, 1989).

Lockyear, H., ed., *A Tribute to Ronald Duncan by His Friends* (Harton Press, 1974).

Moat, J., *Welcombe Overtures* (Dartington Poetry Press, 1987).

Newton, K. M., *Twentieth Century Literary Theory: a Reader* (Macmillan, 1988).

Turner, J., ed., *Unlikely Ghosts* (Taplinger, 1969).

Turner, J., ed., *Fourth Ghost Book* (Pan Books, 1965).

Wahl, W. B., *Ronald Duncan: Dramatist and Poet Interviewed* (Saltzburg: Institut für Englischesprache und Literatur, 1973).

Williams, M., ed., *My Cornwall* (Bossiney Books, 1973).